ball pytho

understanding and
caring for your pet

Written by
Lance Jepson MA VetMB CBiol MSB MRCVS

ball pythons

understanding and
caring for your pet

Written by
Lance Jepson MA VetMB CBiol MSB MRCVS

Magnet & Steel Ltd

www.magnetsteel.com

ISBN: 978-1-907337-67-3
ISBN: 1-907337-67-9

Contents

The ball python

Ball or royal pythons (python regius) are an enormously popular pet snake worldwide – indeed, at the time of writing, this species, with its innumerable variations and morphs, is driving the reptile-keeping hobby forward. In the last decade this small python from West Africa has become a global phenomenon.

Two names, one snake?

In the United Kingdom this snake is known as the royal python, a description that is repeated in its Latin scientific name of python regius, suggesting that this was the original name. The term 'royal' may stem from a couple of sources. The python was known as the king of snakes and a messenger of the god Olokun by the peoples of the kingdom of Benin (now south-west Nigeria). It also seems

Pictured:
The beautiful markings of the wild ball python are in reality disruptive camouflage.

that this manageable-sized python was deliberately kept around some royal palaces as a means of controlling rodents. There is today a Sacred Royal Python Sanctuary at Jefiiri in the upper west region of Ghana.

Another, albeit less believable, story is that Cleopatra used to wear this python around her wrist (obviously the snake's welfare was not uppermost in her mind!).

The ball python name is easier to explain. Most of these pythons when feeling insecure or threatened will pull back their head and throw loops of body over it for protection to form a living 'ball'.

The domination of American literature in the reptile-keeping hobby has caused a progressive change in terminology such that the royal python is now consistently referred to as the ball python throughout the world. This is how the snake will be referred to in this text.

Description

The back and flanks of the wild form of this python are dark brown with lighter yellowish tan spots and blotches along the sides of varying sizes. These may merge or be quite distinct. Often there are smaller dark brown spots present inside these markings that can give the appearance of little alien-like faces! The head is dark brown with a light tan stripe on each side that starts at the snout and sweeps backwards through the eye towards the back of the head. This produces a dark arrowhead-like appearance to the top if the head. The whole underside is typically off-white but can be yellowish.

Selective breeding of ball pythons has unlocked a vast and often stunning array of colour and pattern morphs, which led to the unprecedented popularity of this snake.

Size

Captive-bred ball pythons usually attain a snout-vent length (SVL) of 90cm to 160cm (35 to 63in) and a weight of 1.0 to 2.0kg (2.2 to 4.4lb) or more. The SVL is the linear distance from the tip of the snout to the cloaca – the tail is not included in this measurement. There is a difference in size and appearance between the sexes at maturity – females are longer and bulkier and have longer jaws relative to their body size (Aubret et al 2005). Gorzula et al (1997) found that the wild male ball pythons caught during their study in Ghana had an average length of 125cm (49in), with a range of 100 to 170cm (39 – 67in). Females ranged from 84 to 186cm (33 to 73in), averaging 123cm (48in). They also refer to a huge female, measured at 199cm – six and half feet long!

Average weight was 1.54kg (3.3lb). Wild ball pythons probably take around 3 years to reach a length of 125cm (49in).

Life span

Healthy, well-cared-for ball pythons are very long-lived, with possible life spans in excess of 30 years. The oldest known ball python was allegedly over 47 years old!

Related species

Although the ball python often shares its habitat with the African rock python (python sebae) the most closely-related specie is considered to be the Angolan python or Anchieta's dwarf python (python anchietae) from southern Angola and northern Namibia.

Evolution

Snakes are thought to have evolved from a lizard-like ancestor some time in the Jurassic age (199-146 million years ago, Mya), although no fossils are present until the Early Cretaceous (146 Mya). The extreme changes in body form that are seen in snakes suggest two possible evolutionary pathways. The most likely is that snakes spent a period of time as largely burrowing (fossorial) animals, rarely venturing above the surface. This would have

Pictured:
Wild ball pythons can and do regularly climb trees and bushes.

coincided with the loss of limbs, the loss of eyelids, the marked elongation of the body with increase in vertebrae (backbone) numbers and the re-positioning of the internal organs into this new shape. One species, Najash rionegrina, was discovered in totally terrestrial deposits in Argentina and dates from around 90 Mya. This early snake has a pelvis attached to the spine and possessed fully functional limbs.

The structure of the snake eye is different from that of lizards and may have re-evolved when snakes resurfaced.

The alternative hypothesis is that snakes entered an aquatic phase, and many of the anatomical changes could be considered adaptations to a life in water, although the evidence for this is less compelling.

Pythons were considered closely related to boas, but this appears not to be the case. Molecular studies have confirmed that these are two distinct groups - Booidea and Pythonoidea - and it would appear that shared characteristics, such as large gape size and heat sensor pits, are probably due to convergent evolution. Such adaptations enhance their ability to track down warm-blooded mammals and birds and are probably a prerequisite for the large size seen in some species of both groups designed to take large prey.

At a genetic level all vertebrates – ball python, human or otherwise – possess a series of genes that, in the developing embryo, dictate the types of vertebrae that form and the position of the limbs. These are known as the Hox genes. In snakes it seems that these Hox genes have altered so that the whole body from the first few vertebrae behind the skull to the pelvic area are thorax-like rib- bearing backbones, an evolutionary dodge that has allowed snakes to develop such a versatile body form.

Natural range

The ball python has a wide distribution across sub-Saharan Africa, extending east from Sudan and Uganda across central Africa and throughout west Africa to Senegal. Countries where it has been recorded are The Republic of Benin, Cameroon, Central African Republic, The Democratic Republic of the Congo, Côte d'Ivoire, Gambia, Ghana, Guinea, Guinea-Bissau, Liberia, Mali, Niger, Nigeria, Senegal, Sierra Leone, Sudan, Togo and Uganda.

Natural history and ecology

Ball pythons are usually described as coming from tropical west Africa, but they range through central Africa and into some eastern countries. However, the main exporting countries are Ghana, Togo and Benin.

Ghana has a tropical climate but temperatures vary with the season and elevation. The average daily temperature for the whole of Ghana is around 26°C (79F) and for Accra, the capital, is 30°C (86F). Over most of the country two rainy seasons occur annually, from April to July and from September to November. In the north there is only one rainy season that extends from April until September. Annual rainfall ranges from about 1,100mm (43in) in the north to about 2,100mm (83in) in the south-east. A hot, drying desert wind known as the harmattan blows from the north-east from December to March. This lowers the humidity and causes hot days and cool nights in the north, producing a dry season. In the south of Ghana the effects of the harmattan are felt in January. In most areas the highest temperatures occur in March (average 28°C/82.5F), the lowest in August (average 24°C/75F). Lowest temperature ever recorded was 18°C (64F). Togo and Benin have similar climates.

Habitat

Gorzula et al (1997) describe the ball python as an invasive species that has adapted to the farming landscape of Ghana, where it preys on a variety of pest rodents such as the African giant rat (cricetomys gambianus), the black rat (rattus rattus) and the multimammate rat (mastomys natalensis).

Females have a relatively longer jaw than males and hence a larger gape which may enable them to take larger items. Other prey are also taken, including birds – especially ground nesting species, although ball pythons are excellent climbers, and hatchlings will feed on lizards. One study (Luiselli and Angelici 1998) which looked at both stomach contents and faeces of wild ball pythons in Nigeria, suggests that males feed much more on birds (70% in this study) than females (33%).

Ball pythons generally favour more open landscapes, such as grasslands, that are drier, with plenty of rodents. These provide both a source of food and, with their burrows, shelters too. Forest edges are commonly inhabited. The snakes frequent rodent burrows and termite mounds, and both sexes can be found occupying the same retreat.

However in Nigeria they have also been reported in mangrove habitats (Luiselli, and Akani, 2002), and tree climbing throughout their range is more common than conventionally thought - they may be found resting in tree hollows. Again the tree-climbing abilities of ball pythons are borne out by Luiselli and Angelici (1998) who found that smaller males not only predated more birds than the larger female snakes did, but also took other more arboreal mammals.

Birds and tree-dwelling mammals can be on the menu for wild ball pythons too.

Those snakes under 70cm body-length were found to prey almost exclusively on small birds and nestlings whilst larger snakes fed exclusively on ground-living mammals. It is presumed that the smaller snakes were more able to climb than the heavier, larger ones.

Males appear to be more active than females, possibly because they are roaming, seeking females, or it may be that females move around less because they spend a considerable amount of time either gravid or incubating. This may reflect the higher parasitic tick count found on wild males in Togo (Aubret et al 2005), the more active males encountering more ticks.

In some parts of their range ball pythons are found in areas subject to hot, dry seasons where prey is scarce. In these areas ball pythons may aestivate, becoming dormant and often waiting out this period in rodent burrows. In Ghana, typically this is November to late March.

Reproduction

Gorzula et al (1997) found a sex ratio of 2:1 males to females in their study group in Ghana. It is uncertain whether this was a genuine sex ratio or whether their findings had been skewed by over-collection of females for the pet trade or seasonal variations in the prevalence of one sex over another. In Togo the sex ratios were considered to be 1:1 male to female.

In the Ghana study the population seemed stable, consisting of mainly adults with few young present. This may be because the young are much harder to find or because of high predation rates on smaller pythons. However analysis of their data suggested that less than 10% of adults were replaced every year. Best estimates from the Togo population found that around two out of five females were breeding, suggesting that not all sexually mature females would breed in a given year possibly because a clutch of eggs represented around a third of the weight of a gravid female. Egg production is such a massive physiological investment that in the wild females may be unable to produce them every year.

In Togo females reached a size considered to be sexually mature (around 103cm SVL) in their second to third year. Ball pythons in Ghana start mating from October through to December. Egg-laying is from February to March, with eggs hatching during April and May. Typically, eight eggs are laid but clutches can number up to 15. In Togo mating is from October to December, egg-laying January to March, with young hatching from March to June (Harris 2002).

Eggs per clutch from ball pythons in Togo averaged seven, with a range of four to 15 eggs per clutch.

Predators

The main predator of ball pythons in Ghana is considered to be the Black-necked or Spitting Cobra (Naja nigricollis nigricollis), and locals believe that the 'balling' behaviour has developed as a defence against being swallowed. Other more typical predators would include mongooses as well as raptors such as the Short-toed Snake Eagle (Circaetus gallicus), although the nocturnal habits of this snake would help prevent attack from these diurnal birds. Wild pigs, warthogs and leopards may also kill ball pythons.

Man is a major direct predator of ball pythons, capturing them for bush-meat (food) and skins, as well as for the pet trade. They are also susceptible to bush fires.

Conservation

The ball python is listed on the IUCN list of threatened species as of 'Least concern'. However in some areas there are worries about over-collection, possibly due to the repeated taking of egg clutches from females, for the pet trade. The ball python is therefore also listed under Appendix 2 of the

Pictured:
Cobras are such important predators of ball pythons that their typical 'balling' behaviour may have evolved as a response to them.

Convention in the International Trade of Endangered species of Fauna and Flora (CITES), which sets collection quotas and monitors the number of snakes that are legally taken.

Ball pythons and man

Ball pythons are hunted throughout most of their range as a food source, but they are considered sacred in two areas of Ghana - Afife in the Volta Region and Somanya in the Eastern Region.

Around Afife it is believed by the Ewe people that the ball python represents the spiritual force or god known as Da, which led them from Togo to Ghana about 150 years ago. It is said that if one is killed, it will not rain. Furthermore, if anybody does kill a ball python, they must purchase a new cooking pot and carry the dead snake to Afife for burial in a complex ceremony that requires purification. Ball pythons killed on roads are covered with clothes or leaves as a mark of respect. Although neighbouring villages and peoples may not revere this python as do the Ewes, they will not kill one if avoidable out of respect for their Ewe neighbours.

The second area where the ball python is considered sacred is around Somanya, where the population consists largely of Nyala-Krobo, together with some Ga and Ewe. They have a python festival at

Ball pythons are revered in certain parts of their range.

the beginning of each year. Here too it is a taboo to kill a ball python and if one enters your house, it is regarded as a blessing and a libation ceremony has to be performed.

In Benin there is a similar reverence for ball pythons. Grain is stored in granaries raised on stilts. Not surprisingly, rodents are a persistent problem in these, so for at least the last 600 years local priests have been encouraging villagers to bring ball pythons into the villages as sacred animals. The village python collections and their offspring keep the rodent population down and protect the village grain stores. No python worshiper would ever harm a ball python or think of eating one.

In the west the ball python has become the most popular pet snake because of its manageable size, placid nature, the stunning colours and patterns of modern morphs combined with the reliability of captive-bred individuals. Many imported ball pythons are ranched, a practice which makes them cheaper and has a minimal impact on wild population levels (although there are concerns that it may be having an effect in Ghana). This ranching has made the ball python an important renewable resource for some West African countries. At least three countries – Togo, Ghana and Benin 'ranch' ball pythons. Ranching involves capturing gravid females and keeping them in captivity until they have laid their eggs. The females should then be released back into the wild, while their eggs are artificially incubated and the hatchlings sold for export. At the time of writing, agreed CITES quotas give an indication of the levels of ball pythons exported for the pet trade:

- Togo: 1,500 wild caught and 62,500 ranched.

- Ghana: 7,000 wild caught; 60,000 ranched and 200 captive bred.

- Benin: 1,000 wild caught and 45,000 ranched.

The bulk of these go to Europe and the USA. Indeed there are concerns that, as a result of the sheer numbers of ball pythons imported into the USA, they could become established in warmer regions such as Florida. This has already happened with the Burmese python (python molurus bivittatus) although this large species is better adapted to a seasonally cooler environment than the ball python.

References

Aubret F, Bonnet X, Harris M and Maumelat, S. (2005) Sex Differences in Body Size and Ectoparasite Load in the ball python, python regius. Journal of Herpetology; Jun 2005, Vol. 39 Issue 2, p312-315

Gorzula S., Nsiah W.O. Oduru W. (1997) Survey of the status of and management of the royal python

(python regius) in Ghana .

Harris, M. (2002) Assessment of the status of seven reptile species in TOGO. Report to the Commission of the European Union. Joint Nature Conservation Committee (JNCC), Peterborough, UK.

Luiselli, L and Akani, G. C. (2002) An investigation into the composition, complexity and functioning of snake communities in the mangroves of south-eastern Nigeria. African Journal of Ecology, Volume 40, (3), pp. 220-227

Luiselli L., and Angelici F.M. (1998) Sexual size dimorphism and natural history traits are correlated with intersexual dietary divergence in royal pythons (python regius) from the rainforests of southeastern Nigeria Ital. J. Zool., 65: 183-185 (1998)

Anatomy & behaviour

We all know what a snake looks like. A ball python is a beautiful animal, but it is also a miracle of evolution. So, what defines a snake? The main characteristic is a tubular body, and as part of this package there is a loss of limbs (limblessness), a greatly increased number of backbones (vertebrae) and an increase in skull flexibility.

Tubular body

Snakes have evolved into elongated, tubular-shaped animals, probably to adapt to a burrowing lifestyle, but possibly due to an aquatic phase. A snake is basically a long thorax of ribbed backbones that is both very strong and very flexible. Adopting this body shape has also lead to some rearrangement of the

Pictured:
The heat sensory pits are obvious along the upper lip.

internal organs. These include:

- There is marked modification of the respiratory system. The trachea (wind-pipe) is very long and supported by complete cartilaginous rings that protect the airway whilst the snake swallows its prey.

- Although most snakes have only one lung – the right – ball pythons, along with other python

species, still have two. These are elongated and extend along much of the body length. The first third or so of each lung is supplied with many blood-vessels, and it is here that oxygen take-up and carbon dioxide release occurs. The rest of the lung is more of an air-sac that is used to shuttle air backwards and forwards through the first third between breaths. Snakes cannot cough.

- The right kidney lies in front of the left, instead of opposite it.

- The right ovary is in front of the left ovary in females.

- There is no urinary bladder.

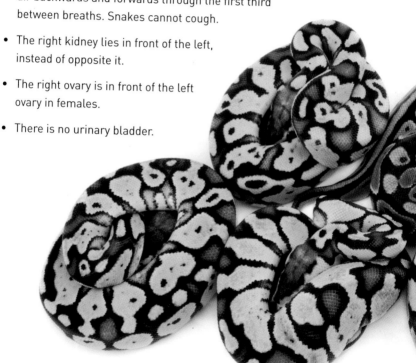

Increased backbones

The number of backbones that make up the whole spinal column is dramatically increased. Ball pythons have some 250 vertebrae. Most of these are rib-bearing and it is this characteristic that gives snakes their flexibility and strength.

Limblessness

Ball pythons have no arms or legs apart from a pair of vestigal pelvic spurs, so how do they move? In a number of different ways is the answer!

There are four types of snake locomotion, known as serpentine, concertina, side-winding and rectilinear.

Serpentine motion involves sending the body into a series of alternating curves, bracing the body against the ground and moving so that all parts of the body faithfully follow the head and neck.

In confined spaces such as burrows, snakes can use concertina movement, in which the body wall is thrown into a series of curves so that the outermost crest is in contact with the surface. This presents a fixed point against which the rest of the snake can be pulled.

When side-winding, only parts of the body are kept in contact with the surface and progress at an angle to the forward movement. This is a surprisingly energy efficient form of transportation.

Rectilinear motion involves a wave of rib movements that propel the snake forward and is particularly practised by boas and pythons.

Skull flexibility

The snake skull is lightly built and can flex at several points. There is a fallacy that a snake can dislocate its jaw. This is not true. In reality the jaw joint is not a simple hinge joint as it is in humans. Instead, there are three bones involved – the supratemporal, the quadrate and the mandible – so that two joints are involved on each side. The two jawbones (mandibles) are not joined together at the front but instead have a stretchy ligamenta attachment.

These adaptations have the effect of increasing the gape by two to three times – an impressive adaptation, but it cannot stop there. Having no limbs means that snakes have no arms or hands to guide or push food into their mouths, nor indeed anything to hold food with in order to pull against to tear it into bite-sized chunks. The snake has solved this problem with two neat adaptations. The first is by developing an extra set of teeth. All teeth in a snake are backward-pointing, and snakes have a single set of teeth on the lower jaw, but two sets on the upper (pterygoid and palatine sets). The second is the increased skull flexibility that means that left and right sides can be moved backwards and forwards independently of the other side. Once prey is in the mouth those backward pointing rows of teeth mean that it is going nowhere except inwards. First one side of the mouth, then the other, is advanced and bears down on to the prey, which is gripped and then pulled back. Gradually, millimetre by millimetre, the prey is ratcheted into the mouth and down into the gullet of the snake.

Skin

The skin of a snake is not necessarily what it seems. The scales are not distinct plates as they are in fish, instead they are thickenings of the outer skin layer – the epidermis – with thinner areas of skin between. Although this is common to all reptiles, in the snake this type of skin has one huge advantage – stretchiness.

When swallowing prey that is often of a greater diameter than the snake, everything must distend to accommodate the meal, including the skin, which stretches at the thinner sections between the scales.

Snakes, like all reptiles, shed their skin regularly as part of the process of growth and skin maintenance; this process is under hormonal control. As with lizards the skin is shed simultaneously across the whole body, but unlike lizards it should come away

as one continuous sheet. This shedding is known as ecdysis and in snakes it also includes both of the spectacles (transparent scales over the eyes which derive embryologically from the eyelids).

At a microscopic level this process involves the following stages and these are reflected in what we actually see with the snake:

- A resting phase. This is the normal state of the skin between sheds. Microscopically there is an outer thickened layer that consists of the skin and scales, with a thin growth layer beneath it.

- When a shed is imminent the growth layer begins to proliferate. There is no outward visible change to the snake.

- The proliferation begins to formalize into a new thickened layer beneath the old outer one. This produces an increase in the thickness of the skin, which we can begin to see as a slight dulling of the skin colours; the spectacles may appear slightly cloudy.

- By the time the newly produced inner thickened layer is properly developed, a thin intermediate layer has formed between the two thick layers. The skin is at its maximum thickness now and so the snake's colours are at their dullest and the spectacles are obviously cloudy.

- The intermediate layer is then dissolved, separating the outer and inner thicker layers to form a cleavage plane. The loss of this layer means that the snake's colours will be seen to brighten and the spectacles will clear.

- Approximately four to seven days after the spectacles clear, the old outer thickened layer is shed, usually in one or two pieces.

Once ready, the snake will begin the shedding process by rubbing its nose against rough surfaces to break the old skin at the mouth and jaw. When the skin is broken the snake will then rub against rough or firm surfaces so that it can gradually work its way out of the old skin. During this process the old skin turns back and may bunch into folds. Eventually the snake will work itself free of the old skin. At this point the colours of your snake will be at their most stunning.

Baby snakes will normally shed around seven to 14 days or so after hatching. The skin of hatchling snakes is chemically different to that of older snakes (Ball 2004) and is thought to be more fluid-permeable and therefore more suitable for life inside the egg; once outside, the skin is replaced by a less permeable one. In fact they will undergo a shed of sorts while in the egg, some five to six days before hatching.

If well fed, a ball python hatchling will shed some six to eight times during its first year and once adult size is reached this will reduce to two to four times per year. Shedding is a function of growth and so the rate of shedding depends upon a number of environmental factors, such as frequency of feeding and temperature.

Special senses

Ball pythons have reasonably good vision. They have no eyelids – instead the eye is protected by the spectacle or brille. Tears are produced and flow into the space between the spectacle and the cornea, keeping the eye lubricated and cleansed. Snakes focus by moving their lens backwards or forwards in the eye, unlike lizards and humans, which deform the lens to alter its optical properties. Ball pythons can see in ultraviolet, which may help in detecting prey trails as well as selecting appropriate basking areas.

Some people believe that snakes are deaf, but they are wrong! It's true they do not have an external ear, probably an adaptation to a burrowing, below-ground phase of their evolution, but they do have a fully functional inner ear. This ear is connected by a series of

Pictured:
A ball python monitors the world around it with the same five sense as we do, plus an extra thermal sense.

bones – in particular the quadrate bone – to the lower jaw, this means that vibrations, even the tiniest footfalls of rodents, can be detected if the snake rests its jaws on the substrate (Friedel 2008). Christensen et al (2012) found that ball pythons are very sensitive to low-frequency vibrations and that any sensitivity to airborne sound is generated by sound-induced vibrations detected in the head – probably via the quadrate bone. This ability enables ball pythons to sense vibrations at very low levels, which doubtless helps with the detection of predators and prey and may be used in communication between individuals.

Therefore a snake CAN hear, and the fact that the two jawbones are only connected by ligaments means that each jaw is relatively free of vibrational interference from the other jaw. The result is that snakes hear differentially between the sides, so that functionally they hear in stereo – which helps to locate prey or potential threats.

Ball pythons have three means of sensing food and other chemicals. These are:

Olfaction (sense of smell) detected in the lining of the nose.

Gustation (taste) detected in the lining of the tongue and other oral surfaces.

Vomerolfaction detected in the lining of specialised

Pictured:
The flickering of this ball python's tongue helps it to pick up scent particles for vomerolfaction.

vomeronasal organs situated in the roof of the mouth. Vomerolfaction picks up non-airborne scent particles from the tongue and lining of the mouth and may play a part not only in food detection but also individual recognition based on a given snake's scent profile.

This may apply as much to how your python recognises you as it does to how it tells other snakes apart. Tongue-flicking is used to pick up these scent particles either from the air or from surfaces.

Thermoreception

Ball pythons have another sense that humans don't – thermoreception. Ball pythons have a series of pits above and below the mouth. These are U-shaped and are exquisitely sensitive to temperature changes up to around 30cm (12in) from the snake's head. Although they are likely to be functional at lower temperatures, their heat-detecting abilities become really switched on when exposed to temperatures above 32.7°C (Gracheva et al 2010), with an ability to detect temperature changes as minute as 0.026°C. Ball pythons have been recorded as responding to an infrared laser within one millisecond. Interestingly, the nerves that supply the labial pits are from the same group as those that perceive touch, temperature and pain, yet it is thought that the information provided by these thermal sensors is integrated in the snake's brain to form a genuine thermal image, like a thermal camera. This makes thermoreception akin to vision in its own right. Eyesight and thermoreception are intimately linked in the brain and it is highly likely that ball pythons use them simultaneously and in a complementary fashion. Thermoreception is used not only for detecting potential prey and predators, but also to select areas of suitable environmental temperatures.

Feeding

Ball pythons are constrictors. Snakes can be highly variable when feeding – in the position they adopt when constricting, the amount of muscular activity they use and the force they exert. Typically, they invoke sideways bends of the front part of the body to wind themselves into a vertical coil around the prey. Three common constriction postures are fully encircling loops that form a coil, partially encircling loops, and non-encircling loops that pinion the prey. Initial tightening of a coil occurs by winding or pressing the loops tighter to reduce the diameter of the coil.

Pictured:
A wide gape means
that ball pythons can
eat sizable prey items.

The most common belief is that constricting snakes subdue their prey with asphyxiation, by enveloping them in a series of coils that prevent the prey animal from breathing. However the pressures generated during constriction by the gopher snake (pituophis melanoleucus) and king snake (Lampropeltis getula) snakes of a similar size to ball pythons have been measured at twice the maximum blood pressure of a mouse. Such high pressures therefore probably kill by inducing immediate circulatory and cardiac arrest, rather than by suffocation alone.

Snakes can probably differentiate between live and dead prey before striking and it seems that factors other than body temperature and movement influence the attack and handling strategies of prey. Snakes do appear to assess the activity levels of their prey (for example, live active vs dead inactive), prey size and strength before striking and will adjust how they will deal with their prey beforehand (Moon 2000). Vomerolfaction may also be important here, with a snake's tongue flicking its prey before capture. They respond most actively to muscle movements by tightening their coils, but also react to breathing and heartbeat. Coil formation is quicker and lasts longer with live prey than it does with dead.

In one interesting study (Heinrich and Klaasen, 1985) some snakes were shown to have left or right-sided dominance when coiling around prey – in other words, some snakes were left or right 'handed'.

Once its prey is dead the snake will begin to manipulate it so that it is swallowed head first, using a number of tactile cues to tell it which way to go, such as hair or feather direction. Smaller items may be swallowed either way; larger may be released with the snake repositioning it if it is going down the wrong way.

Digestion

Pythons are extremely good at digesting their food. It is entirely possible that in the wild, weeks, if not months, can pass between meals so the snake must make the best use that it can of any prey caught. Everything is digested except for rodent hair or feathers. The digestive efficiency of several Australian pythons was found to be between 89 to 98% (Bedford and Christian 2000); the same study found that higher temperatures reduced the passage time and it was suggested that such pythons, if finding themselves with a ready supply of prey, may select a higher body temperature to shorten the time needed for digestion so that they can hunt again. On the other hand, if prey is scarce then they may select a relatively cooler temperature to digest their meal in peace with less energy expenditure. Digestive efficiency is not affected by temperature. But ball pythons love warmth and, if they are kept at too low a temperature, digestion does not occur and the snake may regurgitate.

As part of their adaptation to infrequent meals, pythons have amazing insides – they actually vary in size according to whether the snake has fed or is fasting. As the prey item is being swallowed, the stomach begins to churn out acid to start the digestive process; the pH of the stomach drops from around 8.0 to 1.5 within 24 hours and stays there for around six to eight days to ensure proper digestion. Meanwhile as the prey arrives at the stomach, a sequence of events that help to give these snakes their high digestive efficiency, begins. It involves a lengthening of the intestine and an increase in its surface area for absorbing nutrients. The heart begins to pump more blood to supply these dramatic changes and to aid transport of nutrients away from the intestine. Once digestion is completed these changes are reversed.

Why? Well, maintaining the digestive system in a state of readiness is an energetically expensive thing to do, and a python that may only feed intermittently cannot afford to do this, so this is how they solved that problem. Ball pythons are very quickly able to utilise the energy in their prey. They are able to access it within 24 hours of consumption to fuel their metabolism rather than using up valuable fat reserves unnecessarily (Starck et al 2004).

So this is how pythons can survive for such long periods of time without feeding.

- They have a digestive system that can be kept in a low energy consumption resting state, then switched to maximum effort very quickly.

- They have an amazingly high digestive efficiency that can extract everything that can possibly be utilised from food.

- They can finally down-regulate that system again to a stand-by setting.

Reptiles excrete their metabolic waste nitrogen as uric acid crystals, not as urea as we do. This is the white sand-like sludgy substance naturally present in their urine. It is not calcium, as many people believe.

It can be difficult for reptiles to find drinking water, so they attempt to conserve moisture. One way is by excreting uric acid as a sludge because they lose less water that way.

Snakes do not have a urinary bladder. The kidneys are paired structures situated one in front of the other towards the hind-end of the snake. Urine is formed here and is drained down the ureters into the cloaca. Reptile kidneys cannot concentrate urine, so this is further concentrated by having water absorbed from it by refluxing it back into the large intestine.

As with all reptiles, ball pythons do not have separate external orifices for the urinogenital tract and bowel; instead, they have a cloaca, which is a chamber into which the gut, urinary tract and reproductive tract all communicate. This intermingling of excreta is largely why ball pythons often produce urine and faeces at the same time. The entrance to the cloaca is ventrally at the base of the tail and is marked by a slit-like opening.

Reproduction

Ball pythons are oviparous – they lay eggs. Females have two ovaries, with the right ovary always in front of the left. The female reproductive cycle can be divided into four phases, which occur one after the other. These are:

- Vitellogenesis. This is where the yolk is synthesised in the liver and transported to the ovaries.

- Attractiveness. This is when the female is attractive to males, both by her behaviour and certain physical attributes such as pheromone production, and is sometimes called oestrus.

- Ovulation. The female germinative cells along with the yolks (which combined are called ova) are released from the ovaries into the oviduct, where they are fertilised and covered by the shell to form an egg.

- Oviposition, or egg-laying.

Pictured:
A ball python takes its
first look at the world.

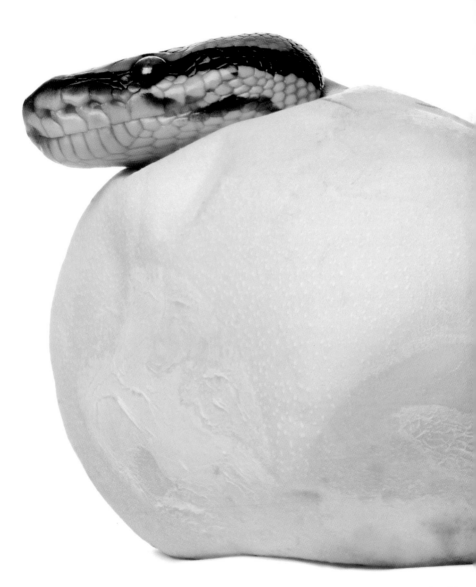

The mating season is the time of year when females in a population are likely to come into oestrus. In ball pythons this is typically October to December, which coincides roughly with the cooler rainy season. Some females may not breed every year.

Males have two testes. In addition male snakes have an extra section attached to the kidney known as the sexual segment of the kidney. This produces secretions needed for mating, in particular the seminal or copulatory plug. When produced this is a gelatinous mass full of spermatozoa that is introduced into the female during mating which blocks the female's oviduct. This plug both prevents other males from mating successfully, and contains pheromones which reduce the female's attractiveness. This plug can last from two to 14 days.

The vestigial pelvic spurs – the remnants of hind legs – are moveable and are used by the male for tactile stimulation during courtship.

Incubation

Ball pythons are unusual amongst reptiles, but typical of pythons, in that the females practice parental care of their eggs. When laid, the eggs are often tightly adhered to each other in an egg mass. Within an hour or so of laying all of their eggs, female ball pythons will wrap themselves around the entire clutch. In the majority of cases the female will completely cover the eggs, and she rotates the last third or so of her body so that the eggs are in contact with her underside.

Ball python eggs are creamy-coloured, smooth and ovoid in shape. They are around 7cm (3in) long and just over 4cm (1.7in) wide and typically weigh between 70 and 100g (2.5 to 3.5 oz).

Every three to fourn hours the female will loosen her coils and inspect the egg mass for up to 30 minutes before recoiling. During the inspection the brooding female will nose through the eggs and tongue flick repeatedly. Occasionally a female may accidentally cause an egg to become dislodged from the egg mass. It will be retrieved by throwing a coil over the egg and drawing it back in. A female will not feed while incubating, but she may leave the eggs temporarily to drink.

Unlike some other pythons, the ball python does not seem to be able or willing to raise the temperature of the eggs more than a few tenths of a degree

Centigrade above ambient. However, females are incubating from January to June in Togo, at a time when there is little temperature fluctuation around 27 to 32°C. Maternal incubation does however reduce water loss from the eggs.

Interestingly, in one study (Ellis and Chappell 1987) the incubation times for maternally brooded eggs was shorter (58 to 59 days) than for those artificially incubated (71 to 76 days). It was also discovered that large egg clutches, where the female cannot completely cover her eggs, are more likely to suffer mortalities due to excessive water loss (Aubret et al 2003).

Following completion of incubation the hatchling snakes will break through the shell wall using a special egg tooth on the tip of their nose to slit the shell. Now able to breathe atmospheric air, they will often rest for 24-48 hours before eventually completing the hatching process. At this stage they have a snout-vent length of around 40cm (16 in) and weigh approximately 50g (2.25oz). They do not feed until after their first post-hatching shed; and typically it will be 20 to 40 days before they begin to feed.

Pictured:
Ball python eggs are
laid and incubated as
a clump.

References

Aubret. F., Bonnet X., Shine, R. And Maumelat S., (2003) Clutch size manipulation, hatching success and offspring phenotype in the ball python (python regius). Biological Journal of the Linnean Society, 78, 263–272.

Aubret. F., Bonnet X., Shine, R. And Maumelat S., (2005) Energy expenditure for parental care may be trivial for brooding pythons, python regius. Animal Behaviour 69, 1043–1053.

Bedford G.S. and Christian K.A. Digestive Efficiency in Some Australian Pythons. Copeia, 2000(3), pp. 829–834.

Christensen C.B., Christensen-Dalsgaard J., Brandt C., and Madsen P.T. (2012) Hearing with an tympanic ear: good vibration and poor sound-pressure detection in the royal python, python regius. The Journal of Experimental Biology 215, 331-342.

Ellis T.M. and Chappell M.A. (1987) Metabolism, temperature relations, maternal behavior, and eproductive energetics in the ball python (python regius). J Comp Physiol B (1987) 157:393-402.

Friedel P., Young B.A , and van Hemmen J.L. (2008) Auditory Localization of Ground-Borne Vibrations in Snakes. Phys. Rev. Lett. 100, 048701 (2008).

Gracheva E.O, Ingolia N.T., Kelly Y.M., Cordero-Morales J.F, Hollopeter G., Chesler A.T., Sánchez E.E.,Perez J.C, Weissman J.S.and Julius D. (2010) Nature 464, 1006-1011.

Heinrich M.L and Klaassen H.E. (1985) Side Dominance in Constricting Snakes. Journal of Herpetology, Vol. 19, No. 4, pp. 531-533.

Moon B.R. (2000) The mechanics and muscular control of constriction in gopher snakes (pituophis melanoleucus) and a king snake (lampropeltis getula). J. Zool., Lond. (2000) 252, pp 83-98.

Starck J.M., Moser P., Werner R.A. and Linke P. (2004) Pythons metabolize prey to fuel the response to feeding. Proc. R. Soc. Lond. B 2004 271, 903-908.

Buying a
ball python

Ball pythons available in the pet trade
are sourced in three different ways.

- Wild-caught. Such ball pythons may be young
  adults, collected from the wild and exported from
  their country of origin.

- Ranched. These are hatched from eggs either
  collected from the wild, or laid by wild females
  that are temporarily held captive until egg-laying,
  before export from their country of origin.

- Captive-bred. These are produced under captive
  conditions usually in the country of sale. These
  may be bred by local hobbyists or commercial
  companies.

Always try to source captive-bred, as these are
usually feeding well, likely to be parasite-free and
will have been subjected to minimal transport stress.

Ranched ball pythons would be your next choice. Although subjected to transportation stress from their country of origin, as hatchlings these may not have been fed and so are less likely to be imprint feeders. When a snake is prey imprinted it will focus only on that particular prey item and will fail to recognise other, apparently suitable prey as food. Therefore a python fed only on white mice may become prey imprinted so will not appear to recognise brown or black mice as food.

Wild caught should be avoided. Ball pythons are not endangered in the wild, but wild pythons are likely to be prey imprinted and may carry parasites, a likelihood increased by being in contact with large numbers of snakes before and after export.

Before you buy

Ball pythons deserve our best care and part of that is preparing for your new arrival. If you have bought this book then this is a very important first step. Read about them. Learn what you can of their care and requirements so that there are no surprises, financial or otherwise. Once you are happy that you can care for a ball python correctly, one of the most exciting parts awaits – purchasing your new companion.

Where to buy a ball python

There are several ways of obtaining your snake, each of which has its pros and cons.

Pet store

This is the most obvious source for a new pet ball python, but there is a wide variation in the quality of snakes and the service that you will receive.

Pointers towards a good shop are:

- The obvious health of the snake (see later in this chapter). This can be difficult to judge because ball pythons do not always display well in shop vivaria. Inevitably they will hide behind vivarium furniture, or are scrunched up in one of the back corners. Always ask for a look at the snake.

- The provision of correct housing. This should be reasonably clean with minimal faecal soiling of the walls and cage furniture. There should be no overcrowding or mixing of species. There should however be some climbing and hiding furniture such as branches and artificial plants. Remember that a shop vivarium setup is different; it is not expected that the snake will live out its lifetime in the shop. The priorities are that the vivarium needs to be easy to clean and the snake easily caught, so a more minimalist approach is often better. Hatchlings are often kept individually in small, clear plastic containers with one end over a heat pad.

- Use your nose. All reptile shops have a smell due to the high numbers of animals, including prey species, which are housed there. However a strong unpleasant smell in the shop often indicates a poor standard of husbandry and, if this is combined with a significant amount of faecal and urate soiling in the display vivaria, then this may suggest a poor standard of care.

- The shop should have plenty of ancillary equipment available for purchase including lights, vivaria, substrate and nutritional supplements. Books and other helpful literature should also be available.

- Knowledgeable staff.

Pictured:
In shops, ball pythons will hide.

If all the boxes above are ticked then it is probably a good place from which to buy.

Internet

Purchasing a ball python via the Internet might seem attractive, especially as the prices are often lower than pet stores, and the variety of morphs wider. You are, however, buying the snake unseen and there is a significant risk involved. Ball pythons that are seriously ill may be sold to unsuspecting buyers by a small number of unscrupulous suppliers, so beware. Buying from the website of an established shop is slightly safer. In the UK regulations govern the transport of all vertebrate animals so your ball python should be shipped to you by an approved courier and not, as sometimes happens, via parcel post.

Private breeder

Buying from a private breeder should mean that you get an opportunity to assess the health of the snake as well as the environment it was reared in. The quality of your ball python will depend upon that of the breeder.

Reptile rescue and welfare organizations

It may be that some reptile rescue organizations have unwanted ball pythons available for rehoming or sale. These will have been assessed by knowledgeable individuals and there will be a significant backup in terms of expertise.

Private sale

A significant number of ball pythons are bought from private homes or acquaintances. This is the least safe means of acquiring a new snake.

How to spot a healthy ball python

Ball pythons can vary in temperament. Adult and sub-adult snakes are usually reasonably amenable to being picked up and examined, but hatchlings can be very nervous. This nervousness can express itself either by the snake attempting to escape when being handled, or by throwing protective loops of its body over its head. They will rarely bite, although the occasional ball python may strike if it feels provoked or unsafe.

Most hatchlings will not bite and even if they do they are unlikely to break the skin of an adult's hand. Do not be afraid – be confident, and gently but firmly pick up the snake.

Handling

Always ask to examine your ball python first, and either handle it yourself or, if you are worried about it escaping (or injuring itself), ask someone competent to do so or have it persuaded into a clear container where you can examine it safely.

For hatchling and smaller ball pythons, gently pick them up by pushing your fingers underneath the body of the snake, allowing it to wind itself around your fingers for security if it wishes. Alternatively keep your hands slightly cupped, with the snake in the centre of your palm. Placing one hand in front of the other will allow smaller snakes to continue to move forward without you having to restrain them. More nervous snakes may make an attempt to get off your hand as quickly as possible (and they can be very quick). Their actions can be controlled by gently resting your thumb on their back so as to slow down their progression (but you are not trying to actually restrain the snake). Do not grip or crush the body of the snake, because this can easily cause bruising and serious injury.

For larger and adult snakes two hands may be needed. First of all push your fingers underneath the front third of the snake so that the 'neck' and first part of the body is supported. As you lift the snake, bring the second hand underneath the rest of it, or the last third or so for larger specimens. Most ball pythons will accept this happily and will often grip the hand, wrist or arm of the handler with their tail and hind end.

Many snakes will seek out warm and dark places while being handled and will attempt to make their way up sleeves, inside collars or any openings in shirts or blouses, occasionally with embarrassing results when help is needed to extract them.

Whilst being handled many snakes will 'taste' your skin with their tongue, using their vomerolfaction to gain more information about you. They may even learn to recognise you this way!

Pictured:
Young ball pythons can be allowed to glide through your fingers whiile you examine them.

Health assessment

Give the snake a general once over. The ball python should feel strong and muscular on your hand or arm, with no tremors, repetitive head swaying or loss of balance. Snakes, like most animals, are symmetrical so any obvious deviation away from this should be investigated. Lumps and bumps are likely to be abscesses or possibly tumours. In particular if the stomach seems swollen and the snake has not eaten within the last twenty-four hours then be wary of the possibility of cryptosporidiosis (a parasitic infection of the stomach). Also check for areas of retained skin. These may appear duller than the surrounding areas, or there may be raised or flaky edges. Pay particular attention to the eyes, where a retained spectacle may be present. Kinked or curved spines may indicate congenital or bone disorders.

Inspect closely for snake mites. These tiny parasites appear as black or brown dots on the snake. Typically they are found in skin folds and crevices such as around the eyes, the corner of the mouth and jaw, and in the labial heat pits but they can be found anywhere along the body. A keen eye will spot a slightly raised scale, and next to it a mite hunkered down and partially obscured by the scale. In large infestations these mites will be so numerous that they can run off the snake on to your hands!

Look for any discharge or obvious wetness around the mouth as this can indicate respiratory disease. Snakes with serious respiratory disease will often mouth breathe, resting with their mouth partially open. Also there are often tell-tale smears of mucus-like material on the inside of the vivarium glass.

If buying a hatchling, always make sure, or ask for assurances, that it is 'feeding well on frozen-defrosted fluffs (baby mice). Some hatchlings are very slow starters and can be extremely frustrating to deal with.

Pictured:
Examine the python's head closely for mites which may be found in the thermosensory pits, or around the mouth or eyes.

Sexing

Sexing is relatively straightforward for adult ball pythons, but not, as is often described, by looking at the pelvic spurs. These are generally larger in males, but they are a secondary sexual characteristic and therefore do not always predict the sex accurately. Large females may have spurs larger than most males!

Male snakes have two intromittant organs called hemipenes. When not in use these lie internally side-by-side along the underside of the tail, and in large males these can be as long as 7.5cm (3 in). Therefore we look for the hemipenal bulges in males, just behind the cloaca. These cause a thickening of the tail in males whereas with females the tail starts to taper relatively quickly. With hatchlings and immatures it is more difficult to judge.

Males generally have longer tails, so if you count the scales along the underside of the tail (known as the subcaudal scales) it is often the case that females will have between 28 – 33 pairs, whilst males will have 32 - 36. The easiest way to count them is on an entire shed skin, but remember that this method is not 100% reliable, especially if the scale count is around the low thirties mark.

Two other methods are known as probe-sexing and hemipenile popping, but neither should be attempted by a novice snake keeper. Consult an expert instead.

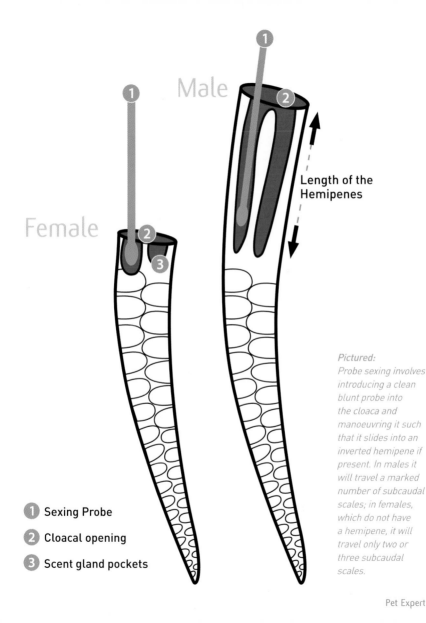

Male

Female

Length of the Hemipenes

1 Sexing Probe

2 Cloacal opening

3 Scent gland pockets

Pictured:
Probe sexing involves introducing a clean blunt probe into the cloaca and manoeuvring it such that it slides into an inverted hemipene if present. In males it will travel a marked number of subcaudal scales; in females, which do not have a hemipene, it will travel only two or three subcaudal scales.

Ball python morphs

One of the most fascinating aspects of keeping ball pythons is the range of colours and patterns available – over 300 – as a result of years of selective breeding by hobbyists and commercial breeders.

The majority of the ball python varieties, usually referred to as morphs, are the result of distinct non-life-threatening genetic changes that cause alterations in colour or pattern. Some morphs are created by combining multiple variations into individual snakes. These are sometimes known as designer morphs and they can be expensive to buy.

The wild-type ball python is a beautiful animal, with an irregular black mesh of markings overlying a golden-brown background. Ball python skin contains three types of pigment-containing cells, and it is variations in the numbers, distribution and quality of

Pictured from top downward: pied, spider, caramel and clown ball python morphs.

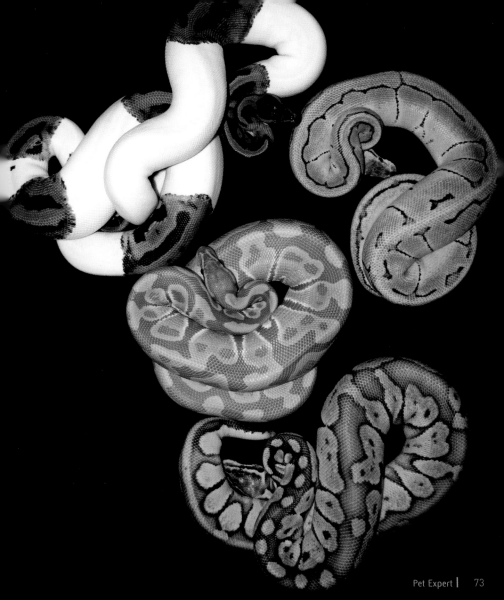

these cells that produce the different colour morphs. These cells are:

- **Melanophores.** These contain black pigment (melanin).

- **Xanthophores.** These carry red, yellow or orange pigment.

- **Iridophores.** These contain crystalline materials that reflect and refract light.

Some breeders favour a classification of morphs based upon the number and type of genetic changes that created them. Snakes, at the moment of conception, receive two copies of each gene (known as alleles) with one from each parent. How these alleles interact with each other can vary and where they are involved with colouring or pattern they can dictate the final appearance of the snake. Therefore morphs may be described as:

- **Single dominant.** These morphs are the result of a single genetic change, and are said to be dominant because the different appearance is still present when only one altered copy of the gene (i.e. from one parent only) is present.

- **Single recessive.** Again, due to a single genetic abnormality, but it is recessive because it will be masked if a normal or wild-type copy of the gene is present. Therefore the changes it encodes will not be apparent unless the snake has two abnormal copies of the gene – that is, one from each parent. Such snakes are called homozygous.

Snakes with only one altered copy of the gene appear normal but carry the potential to transmit it to the next generation. Such snakes are referred to as heterozygous, which is normally shortened to het. Sometimes they are called split instead.

Therefore a normal-looking snake known to carry one gene for albinism will be referred to as het or split for albino. The term simple recessive, as used in this book, means that the gene passes into the next generation as you would expect by standard Mendelian genetics.

- Incomplete dominance (also known as co-dominant). This is when two different alleles of the same gene, each of which would normally produce a certain morph, combine together to give a third, different morph. Actually what is truly incomplete dominance is now commonly, but inaccurately, referred to as co-dominance in reptile literature. True co-dominance is where both allele are expressed and visible simultaneously. In other words the offspring will show the characteristics of both parents. Compare this with incomplete dominance, which produces a snake with an appearance very different from its parents.

- Super is a prefix to describe homozygous morphs where the homozygous version is either an exaggerated form of, or significantly different from, the heterozygous.

- Double trait morphs are the result of two genetic variations. For example one may be giving a particular colour whilst the other a certain pattern. Triple trait morphs need three gene mutations to produce them, and so on.

- Lines. These are where snakes of a particular general type or form have been selectively bred to enhance that appearance.

The full range of morphs is beyond the scope of this book, but the commoner ones, and some of the more interesting varieties, will be looked at. In order to try to make sense of the bewildering array of ball python morphs that are available, an alternative way of classification is offered, based upon four different categories of variation. These are:

- Geographic race

- Colour

- Pattern

- Physical (structural).

Colour morphs

Albino

Albinism is technically a genetic defect; the snake is unable to produce the black pigment melanin the melanophores, but other colours are not affected. However the metabolic pathway that results in melanin can be disrupted at several different points, which in turn can produce different types of albino. The final stage involves the enzyme tyrosinase. Those albinos which do not have a functional form of this enzyme show the classic white background and are termed T- (tyrosinase minus). Albinos which have functional tyrosinase but have a faulty melanin pathway elsewhere are called T+ (tyrosinase positive). Such T+ snakes typically have a degree of melanism that can produce some skin darkening.

- T- albinos have yellow markings over a white background. The eyes, also unpigmented, are pink. This is a simple recessive gene.

T+ albinos include:

- Caramel. Although albino animals are unable to produce a true black, they can be rich in smooth browns, yellows, cream and even a pale lavender colour. A simple recessive.

Pictured:
A T-albino with classic yellow markings on a white background, with pink eyes.

- Lavender. The yellow markings are overlaid on a pale lavender-like background. A simple recessive.

- Ultramel. The normal black pigmentation is replaced by a purple tinge. The eyes are a blue-black with red pupils. A simple recessive.

Axanthic

Axanthic is a lack of yellow pigmentation (xanthophores). Such snakes show a mixture of black, white and greys and, while not colourful, can be startlingly beautiful. It is a simple recessive.

Ghost

These ball pythons are really hypomelansitics and are occasionally called 'hypos'. Hypomelanistic literally means 'less black' and it is this reduction in black pigmentation that allows other colours to show through, so this works really well when combined with other traits. Recessive gene.

Pastel

Pastel ball pythons are stunning morphs that show a high contrast pattern of yellow background (high xanthophore numbers) overlaid with black markings. The belly is white and the eyes are light-coloured. This is an incompletely dominant gene – the homozygous form is known as the super pastel.

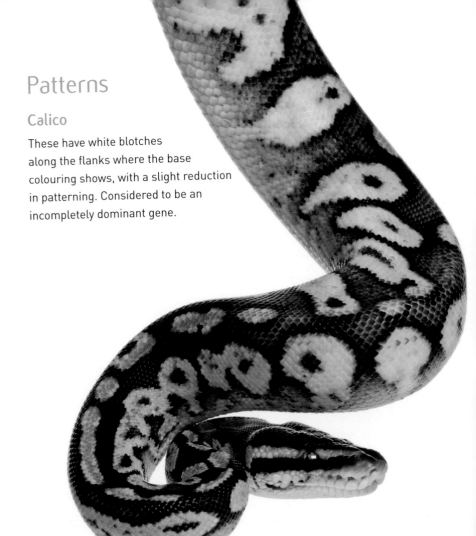

Patterns

Calico

These have white blotches
along the flanks where the base
colouring shows, with a slight reduction
in patterning. Considered to be an
incompletely dominant gene.

Champagne

This is a near-patternless morph
with a degree of dorsal striping that is
also a lighter greeny-brown colour.
Thought to be dominant.

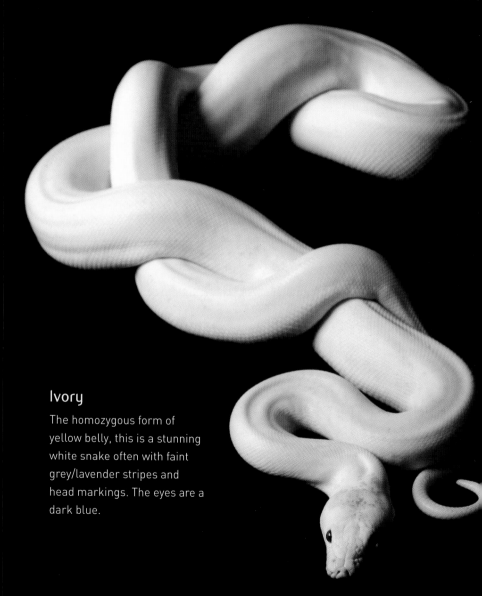

Ivory

The homozygous form of yellow belly, this is a stunning white snake often with faint grey/lavender stripes and head markings. The eyes are a dark blue.

Spider

The spider gene typically alters the patterning into a web-like mesh along the body but can give rise to a range of pattern changes. This can range from a reduction in markings with thin lines on a golden-brown base and white-marked flanks to dark coloured individuals where the markings form a thick webbing. It is a dominant gene that can be crossed with other traits to produce some stunning snakes such as bumble bees (pastel and spider), axanthic bumblebees (axanthic, pastel and spider) and honeybee (ghost/hypo and spider).

Mojave

Named after the desert close to the original breeder's home, the heterozygous morph has altered patterning typified by keyhole-like markings on the flanks. Colour is variable in intensity. Homozygous mojaves are blue-eyed leucistics (which means they have reduced pigmentation). Incompletely dominant.

Lesser platinum

Lesser platinum (also known as lesser platty) ball pythons show a softening of the overall pattern with more brown and yellow tones. Considered an incompletely dominant gene, the homozygous form is a blue-eyed leucistic.

Pin-stripe

These show an extreme
reduction in patterning
down to thin black lines
with white edging.
It is a dominant gene.

Spinners

Spinners are a double trait morph – a combination
of spider and pin-stripe. These pythons have a
markedly reduced pattern with thin pin-stripes and
a yellow dorsal band. Readily combined with colour
traits too.

Yellow belly

This gene is considered an incompletely dominant gene. Yellow bellies have no black pigmentation on the ventral scales and a broken, speckled pattern where the flanks and belly meet. The homozygous form produces ivory.

Woma

Woma is an incompletely dominant gene trait with a high banded but reduced patterning. They were named because of their passing resemblance to the Australian Woma Python (Aspidites ramsayii).

The true Woma python.

Colour & pattern combinations

Blue-eyed leucistic

This mutation is a largely white snake with faint patterning and pale grey head. It is the homozygous or 'super' form of at least two genes – mojave and lesser platinum. Whether these genes are alleles or whether the final blue-eyed leucistic is arrived at by different effects at a cellular level is unknown. An incompletely dominant gene.

Black-eyed leucistic

This is a white snake with no pattern (other than
the occasional pale yellowish markings) with jet
black eyes. An incompletely dominant gene, it is the
homozygous form of the fireball morph.

Cinnamon

Cinnamon ball pythons are a chocolate brown with a white belly. An incompletely dominant gene, the homozygous or super cinnamon is a dark-coloured snake lacking markings; some individuals can be almost black.

Clown

A recessive trait that has a marked dorsal striping but a variable reduction in side patterning. Some individuals are almost patternless. Clown ball pythons are hypomelanistic too.

Enchi

Enchis are named after the area in Africa where the original wild 'enchis' were collected. Initially bred in 2003, these pythons have golden yellow flanks, chocolate-coloured markings and copper/bronze-coloured saddles. There is a reduction in the pattern, although the heads are quite heavily marked. Enchi is an incompletely dominant gene; in the homozygous form it gives us a typical enchi and in the homozygous form (two copies of the gene) we have a 'super enchi' with a further reduction in patterning and a lightening of colour. This trait can be combined with others.

Fireball

Fireball morphs show varying degrees of reduced patterning into a more net-like appearance and a gold background. Considered an incompletely dominant gene, the homogygous morph is the black-eyed leucistic.

Genetic banded

Such snakes have reduced patterning with the dark markings constricted into tighter bands. The genetics of this can vary according to the breeding line.

Genetic stripe

The stripe refers to a complete, or largely complete gold stripe, bordered with darker markings, along the back that is accompanied by a marked reduction in side markings. These snake show a reduction in the intensity of black too (hypomelanism). It is a recessive gene.

Piebald

Sometimes known as 'pied', the patterning on these snakes is unexpected to say the least. Piebalds have large patches of white interspersed along their body, breaking up the more normal patterning. In some cases these white areas coalesce so that some 90% or more of the snake is white. The head however always remains patterned. A recessive gene.

Caring for ball pythons

Correct housing, possibly more than any other factor within our control, will govern how well we can look after our ball pythons.

Previously we have looked at some aspects of the ball python's natural history and how important parameters such as temperature and humidity are to snakes. These vital needs must be addressed. A ball python will not 'adapt' if these are not correct – instead, it will eventually become ill and die.

Many families have only one ball python. They are not territorial, although males may spar during the mating season, and they are neither social nor antisocial, so keeping a single individual will cause it no hardship. However, it is probably best to keep each snake in its own vivarium.

Each individual can then be monitored – for example if there is an unexpected regurgitation you will know

which snake did it. However many owners become so captivated with this snake and the variety of colour morphs available, that many soon end up with a sizable collection!

In view of that, here are some general recommendations on keeping groups of ball pythons together:

- Always feed each snake separately. Ball pythons can become agitated if hungry and may accidentally bite their companions. Also, three sets of backward hooked teeth mean that once a snake has a good grip on a prey item, it can find it hard to let go. If two snakes grab opposite ends of the same prey, it is just possible for one individual to end up consuming the other.

- With large groups, consider providing multiple basking sites so no one animal can dominate this important resource.

- Never mix ball pythons with other reptile species, including other snakes. Ball pythons have fairly specific environmental parameters and if these are not provided then they will eventually become unwell; there is also a risk of disease cross-contamination. This rule can be bent if the vivarium is large enough (zoological exhibit-sized), the other inhabitants need a similar environment

and no one is too small to be consumed, but most of the vivaria available to hobbyists are not suitable for this.

- Hatchlings should always be kept singly.

Here is a checklist for the minimum equipment that you will need:

- Vivarium.
- Heat lamp/ ceramic bulb.
- Protective cage around light.

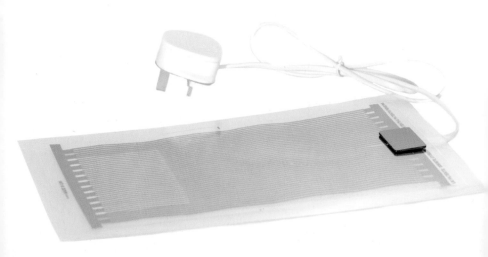

- Heat mat.
- Thermostat.
- Thermometers x 2 (minimum).
- Hygrometer.
- Timer.
- Full spectrum light (optional).
- Substrate.
- Hide.
- Shedding box (at least available when snake is about to shed).
- Furniture (branches, for example).
- Water bowl.
- Cheap diary.

Vivaria

Vivaria are enclosed, often rectangular indoor housings that come in a variety of different materials and styles. For ball pythons, surface area is of most importance, but some, especially males, do like to climb so the vivarium should be a decent height, too.

For an adult a minimum-sized vivarium would be 120cm x 45cm x 45cm high (48 x 18 x 18 inches). Do not keep hatchlings in too large a vivarium; they appear to benefit from the security of smaller containers (possibly mimicking the microhabitats they would seek out in the wild) and they sometimes appear to have difficulty finding offered prey in large, especially highly decorated, vivaria.

Many commercial breeders keep their snakes in a rack system, with each individual kept in its own drawer'. This is a successful way of keeping large numbers of snakes in a small area and utilises the fact the ball pythons enjoy living in enclosed spaces – each drawer is effectively a rock crevice or burrow as far as the snake is concerned. As hobbyists wanting to give our snakes the very best of everything then part of that environmental enrichment should be providing the space for the snake to move, climb and explore. Vivaria that inhibit these activities are just not suitable.

Ball pythons are extraordinary escape artists; they are designed to seek out, investigate and if needs be, pass through the narrowest of gaps. This is especially true of hatchlings. Do not leave anything to chance. If it is possible for a ball python to escape from its vivarium or container it will!

The simplest and least desirable of vivaria are those based on an aquarium or fish tank. Although easy to find, they have poor, top-only ventilation and access that makes them unsuitable. This can make cleaning difficult.

Proper reptile vivaria are much better for captive ball pythons. They are made from many different substances including wood, MDF, plastics and glass that can either be bought ready made, as flat packs or even built from scratch. The potential size and scope of a vivarium is limited only by the available space and the depth of your wallet.

Key features of a good vivarium are:

- Access via lockable sliding doors at the front of the vivarium. This greatly simplifies routine maintenance.

- Water proofing. Ball pythons prefer a humid and warm environment which can take its toll on wooden vivaria. Also, spilled water and urine contamination can lead to rotting wood unless the joints are silicone sealed. If you are doing this yourself, use a sealer designed for aquaria, not bathroom sealants that contain potentially toxic fungicides.

- Ventilation is crucial to the well being of ball pythons. Normally ventilation is achieved by installing grids of mesh or plastic at opposite

ends of the vivarium. These grids are usually positioned at different heights so that as warm air rises it exits from the higher ventilation panel while fresh air is drawn in from the lower. Some of the modern glass vivaria have mesh lids which, when combined with side-opening grills, greatly enhance airflow. There are also small fans available, which can either be connected to a timer, or better still to a thermostat, so that they are switched on when the temperature in the vivarium becomes too high.

- With glass vivaria, opaque strips may need to be placed along the bottom of the sides to provide a visual barrier that the ball python can perceive.

Keeping ball pythons differs from keeping many reptiles because there is no mandatory requirement for full spectrum (with ultraviolet wavelength) lighting for internal vitamin D3 production. It is likely that ball pythons are able to manage without such lighting because they have evolved to by-pass this step. Vitamin D3 is a fat soluble vitamin that is stored in the liver, so eating whole prey such as mice, will normally ensure a ready supply of this important vitamin.

There is, however suspicion that ball pythons may benefit from exposure to low levels of ultraviolet light. They may bask in the evening or morning sun in the wild and ultraviolet light can be reflected into rock crevices and the like, where these snakes hide away, so assuming that they do not benefit from ultraviolet exposure because they are nocturnal may be naive.

Heat

The correct amount of heat is crucially important to reptiles and in the wild this is supplied directly and indirectly by the sun. So perhaps the most difficult aspect of keeping ball pythons (and other reptiles) in vivaria is how to recreate the sun in the box. The sun provides both light and heat. Modern reptile accessories include metal halide lights that produce both light (including ultraviolet A and B) and heat, but as discussed above, ball pythons do not necessarily need ultraviolet lighting and so it is more convenient to separate lighting from heating. This separation of these two key elements allows independent control where necessary.

Temperature

Keeping your ball python at the correct temperature is vital. They have a Preferred Body Temperature (PBT) of 28 to 30°C. Prolonged exposure to sub-optimal temperatures can leave them open to secondary infections such as pneumonia and abscesses. Slight night-time temperature falls will rarely cause a problem, as this is what happens in the wild, but remember that the natural habitat of ball pythons has little diurnal temperature variation.

The temperature at the basking spot should be around 32 to 35°C with a background temperature of 25 to 27°C. Always make sure your ball python cannot directly touch the heat source as burns can occur.

Ball pythons are primarily thigmotherms – they gain their body heat by absorbing it from warm surfaces. Sometimes they bask too, but warm surfaces are their preferred option. Heat mats would therefore seem a suitable choice – they are readily available and are placed either under the vivarium or on the side to provide localised warm areas. They are, however, insufficient to warm a whole vivarium and should be considered as supplementary heating only. They can help to produce warm micro-climates under bark or similar. In smaller vivaria the heat mat should be connected to a thermostat.

A ceramic bulb is better for heating the volume of the vivarium. This acts as a radiant heat source but does not emit any light as a tungsten or spotlight does. Such bulbs can provide radiant heat throughout the day and night irrespective of the lighting regime. Ideally the bulb should be placed at one end of the vivarium so that a temperature gradient forms along the length of the vivarium to allow the ball python to select the temperature it prefers. The bulb should be connected to a thermostat so that the vivarium does not overheat.

Red bulbs are a less satisfactory alternative. They produce heat and only visible red light, which is less disturbing to the ball pythons at night. There are also some blue bulbs available that emit light in the UVA spectrum, also important for normal ball python vision. If using a spot light or other tungsten bulb then this should be on a thermostat too, and plugged into a timer so that the light is not on for 24 hours a day, or, worse still, perpetually flicking on and off as the thermostat reacts to the temperature.

Dimmer (or pulse proportional) thermostats may be better. These adjust the power to the bulb as needed and when switched on, the light will be seen to dim or glow in response to the thermostat, rather than just switch on and off.

Ball pythons gain most of their body heat from warm surfaces, but in the vivarium this can lead to a significant risk of burns. These can be largely eliminated by:

- Heat mats. Do not place these inside the vivarium but use them as described earlier.

- Always place a mesh cage around heat lamps, including ceramic ones. Ball pythons are good climbers and can raise much of the first third of their body off the ground or a handy branch to access warm surfaces – which may include the basking lamp. If the bulb is thermostatically controlled then it may be cool when the snake wraps itself around the bulb, but when switching on it will heat up too quickly for the snake to escape and so it will burn itself. Protective mesh cages are commercially available.

- Hot rocks – imitation rocks with a heating element inside them - should only be used with caution. Ball pythons will rest on warm surfaces to gain heat but if such 'hot rocks' are not thermostatically controlled then the risk of burning is increased. Do not rely on your ball python having the sense to move off before it is burned.

Lighting

In the wild ball pythons are largely nocturnal, although in captivity they can be active at any time of the day. Providing lighting in your vivarium provides a natural day-night rhythm that is important to your snake. It also allows you to see your snake when it does come out and to check that all is well with the snake and the vivarium.

Although lighting is important to snakes, even if only to synchronise it to a natural day-night cycle, ball pythons can be kept successfully without access to full spectrum lighting (that is, light with an ultraviolet A [UVA] or B [UVB] component. However as we have already discussed, wild ball pythons can be active at times of day when they would be exposed to ultraviolet light. Ultraviolet A is probably also important for vision (and therefore how they perceive their surroundings) because ball pythons can see light in the ultraviolet range. It has been suggested that because urine will absorb ultraviolet light, snakes may use their ability to see in the UV spectrum to help identify and follow prey trails.

To give a natural daily light cycle, your ball python should either be provided with a light or be placed somewhere where there is a reasonable amount of light during the daytime (although direct sunlight

should be avoided). Normally the lights should be on for 12 to 14 hours per day, giving 10 to 12 hours of darkness. Day-length may be shortened temporarily on a seasonal basis to encourage breeding.

If you decide to use accessory lighting then buy one of the commercially available units designed for reptiles. Typically these are fluorescent or compact tubes that have been tweaked to produce the important wavelengths of light for reptiles, as well as produce a light that renders more natural colouring. There are fluorescent tubes that emit light in the most important parts of the spectrum, including UVB and UVA. Such bulbs are therefore often referred to as full-spectrum bulbs or lights. If you decide to use such full-spectrum lighting there are some important points to remember:

- Light intensity falls off inversely with distance from that light source, so that if one doubles the distance between the ball python and the light tube, the intensity of the light is halved. This is important as suspending a full spectrum light several feet above a ball python will make its UV output of little use. The ideal distance will usually be recommended by the manufacturer, but if in doubt suspend the tube around 30 to 45cm (12 to 18 inches) above where the snake rests.

- Always position the bulb above the snake. Lighting

Use two hands to support a ball python when handling.

from the side, especially with high UVB levels, can cause serious eye problems. Remember, snakes do not have eyelids.

- Many of these lights are rated according to their UVB output, and this is indicated by a figure at the end of the trade name. Typically these ratings are 2.0, 5.0, 8.0 and 10.0 and 12.0. Each figure refers to the percentage output of UVB and so a light rated as 2.0 should produce around 2% of its output as UVB. Ball pythons should have lights rated at 2.0.

- The shape of the tube affects the area of exposure to suitable levels of ultraviolet light. The compact tubes (which resemble economy light-bulbs in appearance) produce a fairly narrow beam of ultraviolet light while the longer cylindrical fluorescent tubes emit a more even beam over the length of the tube. Ideally the tubes should extend the full length of the vivarium, but if not, situate them close to the heat source so that your ball python will be exposed to the beneficial lighting should it decide to bask.

- Mesh tops can filter out up to 50% of the UVB radiation.

- The lighting is best connected to a timer so that the ball python has a regular day/night pattern.

- Always buy lights specifically designed for reptiles

as many fluorescent tubes said to mimic the sun are colour rendered to deceive our eyes and do not emit the correct light spectrum. Unsuitable lights include those made for aquaria, general fluorescent tubes available from hardware stores and ultraviolet tubes marketed for inclusion in pond filters. These are especially dangerous as they emit UVC and can cause serious eye damage. Glass filters out UV light and so the correct tubes are made from quartz – which makes them more expensive than ordinary fluorescent lights. Unfortunately the UV output declines over time and these tubes do need replacing every eight to 12 months.

Humidity, substrates & hygiene

Ball pythons require humidity of at least 60%, and preferably 70 to 80%. During skin shedding, and the period leading up to it, the skin is more permeable to fluid loss. If the snake is in an excessively dry environment then the old, outer skin can re-attach to the new skin and cause shedding difficulties. Therefore always supply your snake with a shedding box (see page 122) and if the general humidity needs to be increased then regular misting with warm water and a hand spray should be adequate. Commercially available hygrometers for measuring humidity are available – the more useful ones have a digital probe that reads the humidity remotely so that the probe can, for example, be sited in a shedding box. Less useful are the disc-shaped adhesive gauges.

Substrate

There is no single ideal substrate for ball pythons. The commonest types are based on wood. These may be bark, wood shavings or aspen bedding. They are absorbent, so faeces and urates can easily be seen and removed as required. Avoid using with hatchlings or smaller snakes because there is a higher risk of impaction if a piece is accidentally consumed. They also provide some environmental enrichment because if a 2.5 to 5cm (1 to 2 inch) layer is laid down, the snake is able to burrow through the substrate.

Other suitable substrates marketed for reptiles are coco coir and carpet. If you are using carpet, always have a clean, spare piece to replace a soiled one from the vivarium. If using any natural products, remember that if they are too moist from spilled water or urine, they will harbour high levels of bacteria and fungi, increasing the risk of ill health. Always remove faeces when they are seen. Regular replacement of all the substrate will be required.

Newspaper or paper towels can be used. They are cheap but unattractive.

Cleanliness is a serious issue within the vivarium, as it is in any relatively restricted enclosure. It is very tempting to try to set up naturalistic landscapes for ball pythons, but naturalistic vivaria are harder to keep clean because urine soaks readily into the substrate and faeces can be missed. There may even be a disincentive to remove soiled material in case in spoils the appearance.

Furniture

Furniture means providing your ball python with things in its environment that make a home. Ball pythons love to hide but will also climb and burrow. Providing branches and rocks will help to increase their available exercise area, as will artificial vines and other structures. However these snakes can be strong, persistent and relatively heavy so make sure any furniture is robust and well secured.

Hides are essential and can be provided as rocks, pieces of bark, empty plant pots, commercially available imitation dens, often made to look like rocks, plastic and acrylic plants and large pieces of wood.

Another piece of furniture that I would recommend is a shedding box. The idea is to provide a safe place with high humidity where your ball python can shed its skin. They are commercially available, but a functional one is easily made with a plastic tub and lid on. Cut a snake-sized hole in the lid and fill the tub part with a moisture-retentive substrate such as vermiculite, sphagnum moss or a soil/sand mixture. If your female snake is likely to lay eggs then an egg-laying box should be provided too, although in some cases a shedding container may double as a nesting area. And of course, there should be a water bowl in the vivarium.

Pictured: This young albino has recently shed. The shed skin appears in one piece suggesting humidity levels are good.

Care of hatchlings

Many people start off with hatchling ball pythons. They are cheaper, especially for the more sought-after morphs, but do carry a higher risk of problems. They are best kept in smaller, hygienic vivaria or ventilated containers.

Keep furniture to the minimum of a hide and small water bowl/container and keep it on paper towel (or similar) as a substrate to allow easy cleaning. Place the container on a heat mat such that half of the base of the container is in contact with the mat to generate a temperature gradient. Check that the temperatures are suitable with a thermometer and adjust accordingly, either by using a thermostat or by altering the position of the container or vivarium. Small heat mats are available, as are strip-like ones for use with multiple containers.

Routine care

Good husbandry of any pet involves establishing a routine and I would recommend that you buy a small notebook to keep a record of what you do. When cleaning food containers and vivarium structures always use a commercial reptile-safe disinfectant, available from good pet stores. Never use household disinfectants such as bleach. Always keep your reptile cleaning equipment separate from your normal household materials.

Daily routine

- Check that temperatures and humidity readings are in the correct range.

- A light spraying with a hand-held spray will help to maintain a reasonable level of humidity. If possible do this in the morning, in part to mimic morning dew but also to allow surfaces to dry to avoid your snake being exposed to a combination of cold and wet.

- Remove any faeces as you see them.

- Change paper bedding if that is in use.

- Record if fed in your diary notebook.

- Record any shedding or signs of an impending shed, such as cloudy eyes.

Weekly routine

- Thoroughly clean water container.

- Clean glass doors.

- Search for and remove less obvious faecal material.

Monthly routine

- Thoroughly clean the inside of the vivarium making sure that you remove any faeces or urates from the vivarium furniture.

- Weigh and measure your ball python and record in your notebook.

Every six to twelve months

- Change full spectrum lights (if used) whether they appear fine or not. Remember, humans cannot see ultraviolet light. So we cannot tell if the bulbs are still emitting UV light just by looking. Make a note of the date.

- Replace the substrate.

Escapees

Snakes are born escape artists. If your ball python does escape, do not panic. First, try to think like a snake – look for warm, dark niches and holes that it would naturally be attracted to. Unfortunately central heating pipes and openings in floorboards are a bad combination. Ball pythons are nocturnal so set your alarm for the early hours and you may spot your snake exploring. Ball pythons can go without food for many weeks if they have to, so you have plenty of time.

Electrical safety

Keeping ball pythons properly inevitably involves using electrical goods. Always use suitable products designed for keeping reptiles in accordance with the instructions supplied and, if unsure, consult a qualified electrician.

Another potential hazard is electrical tape. Snakes investigate little crevices and this can include loose ends or loops in badly-applied tape. If your snake becomes stuck to it DO NOT PULL THE TAPE, or it will tear the skin. Instead, use either a good, human-safe solvent to dissolve the adhesive, working at it gently using a cotton bud to release the snake. Alternatively, a well-mixed emulsion of water and olive oil can be applied to act as a lubricant.

Nutrition

Ball pythons are carnivores. Primarily they are thought of as rodent predators but their wild diet would also include birds and, as youngsters, smaller prey items such as lizards.

A ball python's prey item can be quite large, relative to the snake's own body, so once it has latched on to prey it will attempt to subdue it rapidly by wrapping its muscular body around it and constricting. This behaviour is hard-wired into the snake and most ball pythons do this whether the prey is alive or dead.

As pets, ball pythons are typically fed on dead rodents which have been stored frozen and thawed before being offered to the snake. Usually these are mice that have been specifically, commercially produced as food for predatory pets such as snakes, other reptiles, and birds of prey. Occasionally, small rats or even dead day-old chicks can be offered too, to vary the diet. Adult mice are pretty much a complete diet as the skeleton contains a great deal of calcium.

Pictured:
Frozen mice are
available in a range of
sizes to suit your snake.

Nutrient content of food

Food consists of a variety of different nutritional elements that need to be considered. These add up to the quality of any given food. Good quality food provides your ball python with the nutrition it requires while poor quality food is either deficient in some or all of these aspects, or else is inappropriate for the needs of the snake.

- Water is an essential part of the nutritional content of food. In addition to feeding the correct diet and occasional misting, clean, free-standing water should always be available.

- Protein is needed for growth and repair of the body. In ball pythons it is likely that some is used as an energy source as well.

- Fat is utilized reasonably well by ball pythons. It is needed especially by reproductively active females, as most of the egg yolk consists of fatty materials, which are an ideal store of energy for the developing embryo. Due to this, the types of fat consumed by female ball pythons may affect the viability of any eggs produced by her. Too high a fat diet (and carbohydrate) can result in obesity.

- Carbohydrates are of minimal use to ball pythons – the only ones they naturally receive would be in the gut of their prey.

- Fibre or roughage promotes normal gut motility and stool formation, both of which are vital to a normal gut environment. Much of the roughage acquired by ball pythons is in the fur and feathers of their prey.

- Ball pythons require a number of vitamins to remain healthy. They can broadly be divided into water-soluble and fat-soluble. The water-soluble vitamins, such as vitamin C and the B vitamin group, cannot generally be stored and so need to be manufactured and used as needed. Fat-soluble vitamins on the other hand can be stored in the body's fat reserves.

- The most important fat-soluble vitamin is D3. This is required to absorb calcium out of the gut and into the body. Without it calcium cannot be taken up in significant quantities, even if a large amount is present in the food. It is produced in several stages. First of all provitamin D is converted to a second compound – previtamin D – in the skin under the presence of ultraviolet light. Previtamin D is then further converted to vitamin D3 by a second reaction, but this is a temperature-dependant change and so the snake must be at its preferred body temperature for this to happen. Vitamin D3 is then further converted into more active substances in both the liver and kidneys.

Because vitamin D3 can be stored in the liver, a ball python fed on healthy mice or rats will gain enough vitamin D3 directly to satisfy its needs.

Ball python food

Mice

Ball pythons are usually fed on mice, the size of which is up-graded as the snake grows. These mice are commercially produced, humanely euthanased and frozen. The carcasses must be thoroughly defrosted.

The different sizes of mouse are usually referred to by their developmental stage as follows;

- Pinkies. New-born mice that do not yet have any hair and weigh up to 4gm. The skeleton of a pinkie is just soft cartilage; the only calcium present is in milk present in the mouse's stomach, so it should be supplemented with calcium. Mouse pinkies are usually too small even for hatchling ball pythons.

- Fuzzies or Fluffs. These are young mice, 4 -7gm in weight. They are just beginning to develop their coats, hence the name. Again, they contain little calcium.

Pictured:
Ball pythons need to be
fed on frozen/defrosted
rodents – in this case a
small rat is presented
as food.

- Hoppers or Weaners. These mice are around 8-10g in size. Once weaned the mice are much more nutritious and a more complete diet for the snake.

- Adult mice.

Rats

Rats are suitable as food for larger ball pythons. Again these are available in a variety of sizes:

- Pinkies/pups. At up to 10g, these are suitable for hatchlings only

- Fuzzies/fluffs/weaner rats weighing 10 to 50g are more nutritious.

- Large weaners range from around 50 to 95g.

- Adult rats.

Other rodents

Occasionally other frozen rodents are offered for sale by suppliers. Potentially suitable ones would include small hamsters, gerbils and multi-mammate mice (also known as African Soft-Furred mice). Never feed wild-caught rodents. These are likely to carry disease and harbour intermediate stages of parasites, plus they may have ingested poison.

Dead day-old chicks

Day-old chicks are a bi-product of the poultry industry. They are the 50% of chicks that are male and therefore not needed for egg production. Like pinkies, they do not contain much calcium in the skeleton, and much of the nutrient value of the chick is in the yolk. Unfortunately the yolk is frequently rancid when the chick is defrosted and so needs removing. A vitamin and calcium supplement should be sprinkled into the cavity left by the removal of the yolk sac. Day-old chicks, at around 35 – 45g, are suitable for smaller ball pythons as a means of varying their diet.

Practical feeding

Prey imprinting

Ball pythons are known to imprint on particular prey items. This may be a particular type of rodent such as multimammate mice, or prey of a particular coat colour. This can cause problems, especially in wild-caught or adults of unknown origin, where the type of prey the snake is habituated to, is unknown.

Normal inappetance

Many populations of ball pythons seem to go through an annual loss of appetite linked with aestivation– a state of relative dormancy associated with dry, hot environmental conditions. This inappetance may last for up to six months, and probably coincides with a seasonal absence of prey. What can be normal for an individual snake can be very frustrating for the snake keeper; often the best indicator as to whether an inappetant snake is ill or just fasting is its body condition. If it loses condition then there is likely to be a problem; if it remains the same

weight or only loses approximately two to three % body weight per month then it is more likely to be undertaking a normal physiological fast. The tendency to undertake this type of fasting is probably genetic, and may also be more likely to happen in wild-caught/ranched or first generation captive-bred. In Ghana there is a dry season from November through to late March and experience suggests that it is during these months that some ball pythons,

Pictured:
Captive bred ball
pythons such as this
pied, may still follow
instinctive seasonal
patterns like their wild
relatives.

especially wild-caught individuals, will cease to feed.

Ball pythons may also fast during the mating season, when gravid or prior to egg deposition.

Size of prey

Ball pythons have a distensible jaw and gullet that allows them to swallow prey many times larger than you would imagine. However, as a general rule offer foods of a diameter one and a half times that of the maximum width of the snake. A little bit larger is unlikely to cause problems, and a bit smaller is fine too.

Frequency

Ball pythons need frequent feeding. Adults should be offered food every 10 to 14 days. Hatchlings and young snakes need to be fed every five to six days. As the snake grows , feedings are progressively reduced towards a more adult regime. Pet ball pythons are quite sedentary compared to their wild cousins and, if fed too often, they can become obese, which can be life-threatening.

Offering food

At the time of purchase most ball pythons will be feeding on previously-frozen mice or rats of an appropriate size. Thaw the frozen rodent at an ambient temperature. Placing frozen mice on very warm or hot surfaces may partly cook them or encourage rapid partial decomposition. If you feel you need to warm up the mouse in an attempt to encourage feeding (by mimicking a warm-bodied prey) try dipping the defrosted mouse into very warm water and drying it with a paper towel.

Some healthy snakes will quickly learn the routine and become quite active at the first whiff of a mouse, and will happy grab, constrict and consume a mouse just laid on to the vivarium substrate. Others are more secretive. These will, however, often feed if you leave their food just outside their hide during the early evening.

Some reluctant feeders may need tease-feeding, but many ball pythons will respond to this as a threat and will merely retract their head into loops of their body. Do not persist with tease-feeding with such snakes. For those that do respond, tease-feeding involves trying to stimulate a feeding response by moving the prey-item in such a way as to resemble the movements of a live animal.

Usually the mouse is held in a set of feeding tongs or forceps (do not hold in the hand as the snake may make a mistake and bite the wrong thing!). Such movements should be jerky and slightly erratic with the mouse at least 10cm (four inches) away from the snake, moving it progressively closer. Remember you are trying to arouse a hunting and striking response; if you bash the snake's sensitive nose with the mouse you are more likely to trigger avoidance behaviour. For real problem feeders, see page 146.

Live foods

The feeding of live rodents or other prey items is unnecessary and risky. It is unnecessary because virtually all ball pythons can be weaned on to dead food. It is risky because mice and other rodents can bite and seriously injure your snake. The only justification for feeding live prey is as a temporary measure to keep the snake alive while weaning it on to a diet of frozen prey. The welfare of the snake must be balanced against the welfare of the rodent.

Feeding problem ball pythons

At one time ball pythons had a really bad reputation as reluctant feeders. Typically these were wild-caught animals that often had significant parasitic loads and were being kept in substandard conditions. Factor into this that ball pythons from some areas may undergo a seasonal loss of appetite and a recipe for stress and worry becomes obvious.

Remember that mice may not be the prey of wild ball pythons, and this may explain why some snakes are reluctant to take them. Some do prey imprint and will only accept certain types of food. Also bear in mind that snakes detect potential prey initially either by sight or by volatile scents and finally decide on

what may be suitable using vomerolfaction of non-volatile scent, often taken directly off the surface of the prey animal itself.

If your newly-purchased ball python refuses to feed within two to three weeks, then I would work through the following actions:

- Review its environment, paying particular attention to temperature, humidity and provision of hides. The temperature in particular may be too low.

- Stop any but necessary handling. Regular handling, especially by inexperienced hands, can be stressful and may add to a snake's feeling of vulnerability.

- Weigh the snake twice weekly and keep a record. Little or no weight loss suggests a normal fast, especially if the snake is adult.

Assuming there is little or no weight loss then a number of techniques to encourage your snake to feed can be employed.

- Warm up a suitably-sized mouse in a cup of hot water, dry it well with a towel and present it outside the snake's hide immediately after lights out, then leave well alone. This will hopefully trigger thermoreception, scent and vomerolfaction to encourage feeding. Repeat over several nights.

Never microwave frozen mice – they explode!

- Do the above but offer the food to the snake in a darkened, enclosed space such as a pillow case, cardboard box or other container. Make sure that the ambient temperature is suitable however.

- Using a set of forceps, treat a mouse as above but dangle it in front of the opening. Some snakes may take it this way, but many will just withdraw in which case do not persist.

- If you think your snake is prey imprinted, either try to offer them what you think they may like (for example, gerbil instead of mouse), or even try different coloured mice. It may be something as simple as offering a wild-coloured mouse instead of a white one. If you do find something that your snake will take, but wish to convert it on to mice or rats, rub a frozen/defrosted/heated mouse over with the prey of choice to begin with before offering it.

- With hatchlings, sometimes feeding can be stimulated by 'braining' a frozen-defrosted pinky. This involves opening up the skull so that the snake can smell/taste brain tissue, which in some snakes can trigger feeding.

- Try over a period of several days before giving up, but if none of the above are working, then live food can be offered.

- For hatchling or small ball pythons, offer a live mouse fluff. It is the movement of the fluff that one hopes will trigger a feeding response. If the fluff is not consumed within 30 minutes, remove it and replace it with a dead one.

- For larger snakes, offering a live mouse or rat pup may initiate feeding. It is risky to leave a live mouse or rat with your snake for any period of time if it is not taken soon. Although a snake is unlikely to be recognised as a potential predator (until it strikes) the high temperatures, lack of food and novel environment may make the rodent more nervous and likely to bite. Rodent bites can very easily become infected, and can be severe in nature.

Also if the snake does not want to feed then a live mouse running around may stress it, triggering hiding/aversive behaviour rather than feeding. Place a live rodent in with your snake during the late evening, when your snake is more likely to want to hunt, but only leave it in there for the maximum of an hour before removing it.

Assisted feeding is absolutely the last resort. It is stressful to the snake and the risk of injury to your snake in inexperienced hands is significant, so if this is needed then seek help from an expert. However if you reach this stage, or if your snake is losing condition or showing other abnormal symptoms, then make an appointment with a veterinarian.

Water

A shallow bowl, dish or water feature, containing clean water, should always be available.

Holiday feeding

Ball pythons, even hatchlings, will happily survive for a couple of weeks without feeding, so should you go on a short holiday, feed them well for a week or two before you go, then leave them to it. Someone should check them on a regular basis however in case of problems, and make sure water is available.

Breeding ball pythons

Once the basics of ball python husbandry have been mastered, breeding becomes the next challenge for many owners. The ever-expanding range of morphs, and the exciting possibilities of what new combinations can be produced, is another huge draw factor.

For ball pythons to breed you obviously need a male and a female. Sexing is discussed in the chapter on buying a ball python (see page 58). The other important factor is that your snakes should be sexually mature. Sexual maturity in snakes is largely weight-related, not age-related. To be sure, typically males should weigh at least 700g (1.5 lb) and females 1600g (3.7lb). Snakes of smaller sizes than these can breed, but smaller males may have difficulty dealing with larger females, and producing eggs may just take too much out of smaller females.

Breeding is potentially a risky time – it places a lot of stress on the snakes and the lowered temperatures (see Conditioning) mean that they have an increased susceptibility to infection.

Communal vivaria can and do work with ball pythons, with matings occurring spontaneously when conditions are right. However, for a more controlled situation, especially for selective breeding, then the sexes are best kept separately to encourage mating when they are placed together.

Preparation for the breeding season

The breeding season for wild ball pythons is from October to December and is triggered by environmental cues, most particularly temperature. Make sure that your snakes are well fed. This applies especially to the female – preparing the ovaries for egg production in females occurs in the weeks leading up to this period; a great deal of nutrients will be transported into the ovaries and then on into the eggs to provide the building blocks for making the next generation.

Conditioning

Reduce the temperature down to around 28°C(82F) with a cool end temperature of no lower than 22 °C(72F). Dropping it lower than this risks immune suppression and disease outbreak.

Shortening day-length gradually from 12 hours to 10 hours can also be beneficial.

Other factors beyond the breeder's control, such as seasonal low-pressure fronts, can also help to initiate breeding behaviour.

Keep offering food, although it is highly likely that your snakes will reduce or stop feeding once this regime is initiated. This is normal and of no concern, even though it might be several months before they begin to feed again.

Breeding

If you have begun conditioning your snakes from October, then November is the best time to introduce the sexes so that the snakes have had some three-four weeks of exposure to their new regime.

Males are best introduced and left in with the desired female for around three days to allow one or more matings to occur, followed by a two or three day break. Sperm is not manufactured by the male at this time – it is made and stored by the male in the interim period since the last mating season. When mating he therefore has only a finite amount, so the number of matings is best kept low to maintain fertility. Breeding with around one to three females is optimum; more, and fertility is likely to be reduced. Some breeders may alternate males to ensure genetic diversity, although if selective breeding is being undertaken usually only one male is used. Females should be mated at least once every shed cycle.

Courtship

Courtship behaviour can begin almost immediately after introduction of the pair, or the snakes may just take their time. Females are especially attractive after shedding as this releases the female's sex-pheromone, to which the male will respond by chasing the female and rubbing against her.

Courtship is initiated by the male and ends at the first mating attempt. Female sex-pheromone is picked up using vomerolfaction and stimulates the conditioned male to begin courtship. Now the spurs are also put to good use by the male, who uses them to stroke the female to help her become responsive. If she is ready, the stroking causes her to twist her cloaca to one side while the male works his tail underneath hers. Eventually the male is able to insert one of his hemipenes into the female's cloaca.

True mating occurs when intromission is achieved, and ends when the hemipene is withdrawn from the female cloaca. Sometimes the male will place a loop of tail over the female immediately in front of the cloaca. This actual mating is sometimes referred to as

'locking'. The pair, if undisturbed, will remain joined for anywhere between three to four hours with some matings lasting up to 24 hours. Be wary however - some inexperienced males will just lie alongside the female and even place their tail underneath that of the female without actually copulating.

Mating usually occurs before ovulation and it seems that females can store sperm for a period of time, utilising it to fertilise their eggs only when they are ready to ovulate. By doing this ball pythons can mate when they have the opportunity rather than waiting for the optimum time when a member of the opposite sex may not be available.

Practical breeding

Under environmentally appropriate conditions, reproductively active females will begin developing ovarian follicles in readiness for egg production. During this time behaviour and body shape begins to change.

A female will begin to seek cooler temperatures and may wrap herself around the water bowl. She may also twist her back half so that her back is in contact with the substrate. It is speculated, but unproven, that this may help with localised thermoregulation of the ovaries.

As ovarian development progresses physical changes become obvious too, and many breeders refer to this as 'building'. This lasts for around two weeks prior to ovulation. Some females develop a kinked appearance to the last third of their body prior to ovulation, whilst others will show a temporary thinning or side deviation of the tail that breeders call 'tail suck'. The female's colouring may change too, becoming lighter and brighter. An individual female may show some, all or none of these signs! Several breeders now use ultrasound scanners to confirm which females are showing ovarian development. Why the emphasis on ovulation? Male snakes have only a certain amount of sperm stored for use during the breeding season and most breeders are not prepared to let their often valuable males waste it on speculative matings.

With well-conditioned females, ovulating ball pythons can be identified by the pronounced swelling of the back half of the body as the ovaries enlarge. The ventral scales may also show more curved bulges at that point too. It may look as though she has swallowed a large meal.

This is the time to pair her with a male. However this body swelling only lasts around 24 hours and can easily be missed. Once she has ovulated she will return to her more normal shape because all those ripe ovae are no longer bunched together on the ovaries. Instead, the ova make their way down and along the reproductive tract where they are fertilised by the male's sperm, outer membranes are placed around them and finally a leathery shell added by the shell gland to form the final egg.

Where possible remove any branches or similar furniture from naturalistic vivaria. On occasion some females may decide to wander off or climb whilst the pair are still joined and in some cases this can cause damage to the hemipene of the male. Often these can be slow or unable to retract. In such cases, if the hemipene appears unharmed then removing the male to a clean environment such as an acrylic vivarium without substrate, but with a hide, will often see the hemipene retracted uneventfully. If this has not occurred within a couple of hours, or if the hemipene is traumatised and bleeding, then seek veterinary help. Even if amputation of the hemipene is required this is not a disaster – the male has another hemipene on the other side and so will still be able to breed in the future.

Egg-Laying

Around 14 to 16 days after ovulation the female will shed her skin. Make a note of this in your diary as around 21-28 days later she will be due to lay. At this time make sure that the humidity is kept high – at least 70%. Following this shed, a now-gravid female will begin to seek warmer temperatures, curling up over the hotspot, raising her body temperature higher to encourage embryonic development.

Whilst some females will feed right up until egg-laying , many others will not feed at all and will begin to loose condition as time passes. Muscle mass is broken down by the snake as an energy reserve, which makes the backbone more obvious and gives the snake a slightly malnourished appearance.

When it comes close to egg-laying, a gravid female will begin to look for somewhere warm, humid and secure – in other words, somewhere where she can incubate her eggs safe from potential predators, so it is usually best to provide an egg-laying box.

This is much like a shedding chamber. Use an appropriate-sized plastic container and cut a hole in the top sufficient for the female, with her increased girth, to enter. Use a moisture-retentive substrate that will make it humid, but not wet. Moss works well; vermiculite

can be used but tends to stick to the snake. The female will enter this container and push and shove the nesting material around to create a space within which she feels secure enough to lay her eggs.

Ball python breeding strategy is to produce a small number of large eggs, and to increase the chance of the young surviving by actively incubating and protecting them, unlike other snakes, such as corn snakes, whose responsibility ends after egg-laying. Typically a female ball python will lay 3 to 8 eggs although large females may produce one or two more. Each egg should weigh between 90 to 140g (3 to 5oz), although they can be as small as 75g and still be fertile. The eggs will usually adhere to each other, forming a fairly solid egg mass. Within an hour or two of completing the egg-laying the female will wrap herself around the clutch and begin incubation.

Healthy eggs will be soft initially but will harden up and appear quite white or slightly yellowish with a firm, leathery texture. Infertile ones tend to be smaller and more yellow and frequently do not adhere to the rest of the clutch.

The most that one can hope for is one clutch of eggs out of every female per breeding season. Maternal investment in eggs is high and it can really take it out of the female. Once the clutch has been removed (or has hatched, if she is allowed to incubate the eggs herself) then return her to optimum conditions. Most females will begin to feed readily at this point.

Incubation

In principle the ball python breeder now has a choice of whether to leave the eggs with the female and allow natural incubation to take place, or to remove the eggs for artificial incubation. In practice most breeders will remove the eggs.

Natural incubation

If the eggs are to be left with the female then keep the temperature at around 30 to 31°C with a slight night-time drop. Handle the female as little as possible during this period and do not offer food; she will not feed while incubating and to offer food will only stress her.

Egg removal

If the eggs are to be artificially incubated then they need to be removed within 24 hours of laying. This is because inside the egg the embryo (which at this stage consists of only an aggregate of cells), gradually migrates up to the highest point of the shell so that it eventually comes to sit on top of the yolk. After 24 to 48 hours it attaches to the inner cell membrane - the allantois. This membrane is important for oxygen uptake and carbon dioxide release, calcium absorption from the shell and storage of harmful waste products. This connection is essential but is, to start with, very fragile. Any rotation of the egg within the period of 24 hours after laying to around 20 days of incubation is liable to sheer off the embryo and cause its subsequent death.

Female ball pythons will actively guard their eggs, although the degree of enthusiasm for this varies between individuals. Many females will strike at hands. With one hand, grasp the female behind the head and with the other the tail, gently unwinding her body from around the clutch from the tail forwards. Be gentle and make sure you unwrap the female from the eggs – the eggs will be stuck together and if accidentally lifted en masse they can all be dropped. If the female is large then a second person may be needed to ensure smooth egg retrieval.

Once the eggs are safely removed wash both the female and the vivarium/egg-laying box with a reptile-safe cleanser. This appears to remove the scent of the eggs from the snake and her environment and will often allow the female to resume normal feeding quickly.

When handling eggs always be careful not to rotate them. Mark the top of each egg with a dot from a permanent marker pen, pencil or similar so that you always know which way is up. The bulk of the clutch is likely to be stuck to the bottom of the egg-laying box or container and will need to be gently prized from it.

Fertile eggs maintain a turgid appearance during incubation and this can be one way of deciding whether your eggs are fertile or not. Another is by candling. This involves shining a very bright light through the egg. If there is a sizeable embryo present it will be seen as a shadow and sometimes the blood vessels lining the inside of the shell can be picked up earlier in incubation. However, often a shadow is not visible until almost the end of incubation – possibly because it is only by this point that the developing snake is dense enough to block any light. Do not rotate the egg while handling it. Infertile eggs will become covered in a mould and will collapse and shrivel. If it is loose from the main egg mass then remove it, but usually such eggs have no effect on the other eggs, so it is of no concern.

Practical incubation

An incubator should be prepared a day or two before the expected laying date. Ball python eggs, unlike bird eggs, do not need to be turned, so this makes using an incubator relatively straightforward. Commercial reptile incubators and incubator kits are available, but should you wish to make your own then any heat resistant container will do, although it will need to be of a reasonable size to accommodate a pyramid-like clutch of eggs. Remember, the eggs of ball pythons are hard to separate individually, although it can be done with care. The necessary heat source can be a small light bulb, a ceramic heater or a vivarium heat mat that is connected to an accurate thermostat. The temperature probe of the thermostat should be laid next to the eggs. An accurate thermometer is also required (to double check on the accuracy of the thermostat), plus a hygrometer to measure humidity. These are available from garden centres and specialist reptile outlets. The use of a small fan helps to create a more even temperature distribution.

The incubator must not be permanently sealed, as some air exchange is necessary, even if this is only by lifting the lid once daily to check on the eggs. Place some clean water retentive substrate such as vermiculite or perlite (available from garden centres) into this tub. Add just enough water to make it damp, but not soaking. Then create a shallow depression in the substrate and place the clump of eggs into it. Place a card or other label with the morph or parental cross/I.D. and date of lay in the same tub.

Incubation period

Incubation lasts around 52 to 60 days. Fertile eggs stay firm and turgid until around half way through incubation when a dimpling of the eggs can be seen as yolk is absorbed by the embryo. There is often an increase in condensation inside the incubator from this point onwards due to the higher respiratory rate of the rapidly-developing embryos.

Apparent infertility

Adult ball pythons may be infertile for a variety of reasons that may need investigation. Initial starting points are confirming the sex of your breeder snakes and making sure that they are large enough to be sexually mature.

Failure to hatch/dead in shell

There are many reasons why ball python eggs do not hatch. In the first instance consider the following:

1. Temperature. Temperatures too high or too low can lead to embryonic death.

2. Humidity should be monitored and maintained at 90-95%. A very low humidity or a high airflow over the eggs can lead to an excessive loss of water, leading to dehydration and embryonic death. An egg that loses 25% or more of its weight during incubation is unlikely to hatch.

3. Oxygen and carbon dioxide levels. Remember that a ball python developing inside the egg does breathe – not through its lungs, but across the eggshell. On the inside of the shell are membranes well supplied with blood vessels that pick up oxygen through microscopic holes in the shell and simultaneously disperse carbon dioxide the same way.

In sealed incubators or in containers housed inside larger incubators, oxygen levels may fall and carbon dioxide levels rise to dangerous levels. Briefly opening such incubators once daily or every other day will prevent this from happening.

Hatching

Around the last two weeks or so of incubation, the eggs will appear to slightly collapse, but this is normal. It is due to absorption of the yolk sac by the hatchling, and weakening of the shell wall as calcium deposits are also utilised. There is a small "egg tooth" on the nose of the hatchling ball python, and it uses this to wear its way through the shell, creating a slit. Often, once the shell is punctured and a small slit made, the snake may take a rest. It can take up to 36 hours for a hatchling to make its way out of the egg, but eventually it will emerge, a perfect miniature of the adult. Typically, hatchlings weigh between 65 and 90g and have a total length of around 30 to 45cm (12 to18in).

Occasionally some hatchings will appear to have trouble getting out of their shell. It is tempting to help them, but be careful. Hatchlings often have large yolk sacs still that have not been absorbed, and the blood vessels lining the inside of the shell are still functional. It is very easy to damage these structures, with a serious risk of haemorrhage or wounding.

Rearing

Remove the hatchlings into individual containers, but do not offer food as the young will not feed until after their first shed. This occurs some seven to 10 days after hatching. Once feeding, the rearing of hatchling ball pythons is fairly straightforward. Please refer to the relevant sections in the chapters Caring for ball pythons and Nutrition.

A word of warning

There are a small number of hobbyists who set out to breed ball python morphs for financial reasons. Many morphs are very expensive, with some costing thousands of pounds. However there is no substitute for experience and this can only be gained on a day-by-day basis. Selective breeding requires the space to house both breeding stock and raise young snakes to reproductive age, and these snakes must be fed and watered and kept at the correct temperature.

Ball pythons do not always play ball – sometimes they will not breed. It may be that their environment is wrong or they may be infertile, but they still need feeding and looking after.

Be selective about how you source your ball pythons. A common route to riches is to buy an expensive male morph and mate it with as many cheaply-available wild-type females as possible. Females sourced from pet shops and 'free ads' may not be the bargains they appear, as their previous husbandry and nutrition may make them less likely to breed and they may carry disease. Please remember that the highly expensive male morph bought for breeding from an established breeder is unlikely to have encountered any of the commoner types of bacteria and is much more likely to succumb to respiratory disease.

In addition, because selective breeding often involves the breeding of related individuals, some lines may have a weak immune system too, as an unexpected consequence of such breeding.

In summary, if you are a new to ball pythons give yourself a year or two to gain experience, make sure that you have a certain amount of capital in reserve for unexpected expenditure and be careful where you obtain your breeding stock. Find yourself an experienced reptile veterinarian and call him or her in sooner rather than later.

Health

Captive-bred ball pythons bought from a reliable source are usually relatively trouble-free pets. However ball pythons that are unwell are best isolated and kept in hygienic-style vivaria where their environment can be controlled appropriately. Ideally, use only newspaper or paper towels on the bottom so that it can be cleaned out readily, and make sure that any vivarium furniture such as hides and branches can either be sterilized or thrown away if soiled.

If your ball python is especially weak, remove any perches as it may fall, potentially injuring itself. In addition to this the basic care for an unwell snake should include the following:

- Provision of a stress free environment.

- An appropriate temperature of around 28°C, and a hot spot of between 30 and 32°C. A ball python's

immune system will not function correctly if it is kept at too low a temperature. Also, if your snake is on medication such as antibiotics, keeping it at its preferred body temperature will mean that its body manages and eliminates the drug in a manner predictable to your veterinary surgeon.

- Keeping the snake well hydrated is essential. Many ball pythons will lick water if it is gently applied to their mouths with a syringe or dropper.

- It is common for sick snakes to go off their food. Assisted feeding has its place but should not be rushed into as it is potentially stressful and can be damaging to your snake if not undertaken correctly. For larger snakes, stomach tubing may be appropriate. If you feel that this is required consult an experienced reptile veterinarian or herpetologist for instruction.

If you have concerns, arrange a consultation with your veterinarian so that your ball python can be examined and its problems analysed and dealt with professionally. Some of the commonest and important problems are outlined below.

Inappetance

A loss of appetites is often of grave concern to ball python owners, yet it can be normal. Sexually active or gravid snakes often fail to feed, and this can go

on for several months. As discussed, a good rule of thumb is to monitor the snake's weight on a weekly basis. However, if your python is losing more than seven to eight percent bodyweight per month or is showing obvious signs of ill health, have it checked by your veterinarian. Refer to feeding problem ball pythons in the Nutrition chapter if necessary. (page 146).

Inclusion body disease of boids

Usually shortened to IBDB or IBD, this disease is becoming more prevalent throughout collections of boas and pythons. Clinical signs include some or all of the following: chronic regurgitation, nervous disorders (usually characterised by star gazing, loss of balance, tremors, loss of orientation and paralysis) with an increased susceptibility to secondary infections due to immune system suppression and an increase in neoplasia (cancers).

Recent research has shown IBDB to be an arenavirus.

Outbreaks are anecdotally linked with snake mite infestations and it may be that the disease-causing organism is spread by these blood sucking mites (see snake mites later). The inclusions that give IBDB its name are found inside infected cells and are seen on microscopic examination. Identifying these inclusions on samples taken either from biopsies or post-mortems is at present the best means of diagnosing this condition.

There is no cure and it is invariably fatal. Infected snakes in a collection represent an unacceptable risk to the rest and are best euthanased.

Abnormal shedding

Sometimes shedding does not happen normally. This is known as dysecdysis. In most cases it is an environmental problem, and the commonest causes are:

- Low humidity. During the shedding process the skin is very susceptible to water loss and if the humidity is too low then patches of the old outer layer will stick to the new inner layer causing problems with shedding.

- No or inappropriate cage furniture. Snakes need something to rub against to initiate the shedding process.

- Concurrent disease. Snake mites, cuts, scars and other skin problems can cause shedding difficulties.

- Hormonal disorders. These are occasionally seen in older ball pythons.

Managing a problematic shedding involves improving your snake's environment and some nursing care. Make sure that you provide a shedding box to give your snake a secluded, high humidity environment in which to shed, plus a branch or stone against which it can rub.

Regular misting of the vivarium will increase the local humidity too. There are commercially available products designed to aid the loosening of retained sheds which can be tried. If there are patches of shed skin still attached, moisten the affected areas with lukewarm water to loosen the retained skin. Allowing the snake to swim in a lukewarm bath will help too.

Gently grasp and remove any flaps of skin, but if the skin is firmly adhered do not continue to pull – instead, remoisten and try again. If it is persistent, or if the skin is becoming bruised or damaged, stop and seek veterinary assistance.

If a spectacle (see section on Special Senses) is retained this is best removed using a damp cotton bud. Gentle rolling and rubbing whilst applying slight pressure with a damp cotton bud should eventually cause some rucking of the spectacle and allow its removal. DO NOT PULL WITH TWEEZERS OR FORCEPS as you risk permanently damaging the underlying cornea with a consequent loss of the use of that eye. Again, if in doubt, seek veterinary assistance.

Snake mites

Snake mites (ophionyssus natracis) can be a difficult problem to deal with. The most likely source of infestation is the place from which you bought your snake (these are specific reptile parasites) although using second-hand equipment, such as wooden vivaria or previously-used branches, is another possibility.

Snake mites are small (1mm), usually black or dark brown. They feed on your snake's blood and tend to accumulate under the scales, around the eyes, the heat sensitive pits, and any skin folds around the mouth or cloaca. An infested snake may spend much of its time submerged in its water bowl, except for its nostrils. Snake mites have been linked to transmitting other infections, including septicaemia.

The main problem with snake mites is that they are parthenogenic - like aphids, females can reproduce without the need for a male - so numbers can rapidly build up in vivaria. Treatment must therefore include the thorough cleansing of all affected vivaria. What cannot be sterilised with a mild bleach solution (5mls per gallon) must be disposed of. In addition one should:

- Seal any joints in wooden vivaria (using aquarium silicone sealer) as this is where the mites hide and breed. Do not use bathroom sealants as these contain potentially harmful fungicides.

- Replace the usual substrate with paper (changed daily).

- Repeated washing the vivarium with warm water will physically remove any mites.

- Application of topical fipronil spray (available as a flea treatment for dogs and cats) once weekly for at least four weeks. This is best first applied to a cloth and rubbed over the entire surface of the snake. Fipronil can also be used to treat the environment.

- Alternatively consult your veterinarian for an injection of ivermection at 200μg/kg every two weeks will kill those that feed on the snake (note ivermectin is toxic to indigo snakes and chelonia).

- Cultures of predatory mites (Hypoaspis miles) are commercially available for use in vivaria. These prey upon the snake mites, controlling their numbers and possibly eliminating them. These are useful for complex display vivaria where thorough cleaning is not possible, or where insecticidal/acaricidal agents cannot be used.

Ticks

Ticks are much larger versions of mites and can be several millimetres long. They are most likely to be seen on wild-caught and farmed ball pythons. They are usually found along the length of the back and on the abdominal side of the trunk. Less often they may be attached close to the cloaca, around the eyes, nasal opening and elsewhere on the head.

When ticks attach they burrow their head and mouth-parts into the skin of the snake. They can be removed using a commercial tick-remover (remember to twist as you pull to disengage the mouthparts!). Alternatively your veterinarian can inject the snake with ivermectin, which will kill the ticks and facilitate their removal a day or so later.

Burns

Ball pythons are termed thigmotherms, which means that they gain most of their body heat from contact with warm surfaces. Unfortunately powerful unprotected heating equipment can cause severe localized burns. This is a serious problem that you need to consult your veterinarian about as the burn will need cleaning (possibly under a general anaesthetic) and covering, and antibiotic and/ or antifungal medication given. If the burns are extensive then fluids may be needed.

Scars will eventually result which may lead to localised areas of dysecdysis and if the scarring is extensive it may lead to other problems. For example, restrictive scarring may mean that constricting snakes have difficulty completing the behavioural sequence necessary for normal feeding.

Flagellates

These are tiny, single-celled gut parasites that can be a cause of loose stools in snakes. Under the microscope they appear as numerous motile pear-to circular-shaped protozoa. Consult your veterinarian for treatment with metronidazole.

Vomiting/ regurgitation

Persistent vomiting or regurgitation can be a symptom of a wide range of problems. First, make sure that the temperature is correct, and that any prey items fed are in a suitable state to be offered. Frozen prey that has been partially thawed and refrozen may harbour bacteria and bacterial toxins that are dangerous to the snake when eventually fed.

If no environmental or management cause can be found then consult a veterinarian. Other possibilities include, but are not limited to, bacterial infections, foreign bodies, tumours, cryptosporidiosis (see later), IBDB and other gut parasites.

Obesity

Ball pythons, especially females, are prone to obesity, largely due to over-feeding. Taking prey is one of the most exciting behaviours that a ball python can demonstrate and some owners over-feed to repeat the spectacle. Remember that the energy requirements for a ball python are a fraction of that required for a similar-sized mammal, because a ball python is not expending energy keeping warm. Also the calorific needs of a captive ball python, with its privileged life-style, is less than a wild one.

An obese ball python has a gross, swollen appearance to its body and the head may appear unnaturally small. In extreme cases fat may appear partially sectioned, giving a 'string of doughnuts' appearance.

Aim for a gradual weight loss by reducing feeding frequency or size/number of prey items, and follow the normal feeding guidelines in the Nutrition section. However just opting for long-term starvation is likely to generate serious problems. Supplement with vitamin E to reduce the risk of steatitis (inflammation/rancidity of stored body fats).

Cryptosporidium

Crytosporidium serpentis is a real problem if it gets into your snake collection. It is a protozoal parasite, the most obvious sign of which is a grossly abnormal thickening of the stomach wall. Hence it is sometimes referred to as hypertrophic gastritis. Crytosporidium causes regurgitation, extreme weight loss, depression, mucus-laden stools and an obvious abdominal bulge caused by the thickened stomach.

Cryptosporidium has a direct life cycle; infection is by exposure to water containing infective cysts. It is not carried by rodents.

There is no recognised effective treatment although some regimes may help, so consult your veterinarian if you are worried by this problem. It is persistent too, with cysts remaining viable in water for up to seven months at 15°C. Disinfect the vivarium and equipment by exposing to water above 64°C for longer than two minutes. Crytosporiduim cysts are very resistant to chlorine or iodine.

Bacterial infections

These are often secondary to another problem, so investigation of underlying factors should be encouraged. Typically, infections are the result of poor immunity (consider inappropriate temperatures, poor nutrition etc) or breaches of the skin such as cuts, bites from live prey or other snakes, or mite-bites. Damp or wet environments can also lead to blisters and sores, especially on the ventral scales (known as Ventral Dermal Necrosis, Vesicular Dermatitis or Blister Disease).

Septicaemias present with bruise-like haemorrhages in the skin and the snake may display abnormal behaviours.

Ventral Dermal Necrosis appears as blisters and sores and may rapidly progress to a septicaemia. Any swelling, especially in the skin, should be considered a possible abscess.

Your veterinarian will treat with antibiotics and other supportive care may be needed. Blisters and sores may need treatment along the lines of burns described above and healing of these can be prolonged. An abscess may require surgical removal.

Pneumonia

Pneumonia is a common and serious problem in ball pythons. It is often encountered in snakes that are breeding and subjected to the triple risk of high stress levels, raging sex hormones and relatively low temperatures, all of which can significantly suppress the immune system.

In addition, when paired with new females, males may be exposed to bacteria that their immune system has never encountered before.

Often the first sign is finding mucus smeared on the inside of the vivarium. Snakes will open mouth breathe, often with the windpipe extended and fully dilated, as they struggle to gain oxygen. A rattling sound may be heard and a mucous discharge may be found in and around the mouth.

The anatomy of the lung an the long, narrow windpipe make coughing, and therefore the removal of infected material out of the lungs, a very difficult and potentially fatal problem. Some snakes will suffocate with a plug of thick mucus in their trachea.

Antibiotics are essential, as is good husbandry. Your veterinarian may need to submit samples to a laboratory to find out what the infection is and which antibiotics are appropriate. Occasionally there are other causes of pneumonia such as fungal infections or ophidian paramyxovirus.

Stomatitis (mouth rot)

Usually a bacterial infection but it can be fungal. Typically one sees inflammation of the oral membranes that may progress to ulcers. Layers of thick pus-like material may be present. The snake may well be salivating.

Occasionally, infection may track up the lachrymal duct, resulting in a sub-spectacular abcess over one or both eyes.

Snakes may not feed whilst suffering from stomatitis, so the snake may require fluid and nutritional support, given via stomach tube, during this time.

Note that the stomach tube should be lubricated and coated with appropriate antibiotic to try to prevent spread of infection to the oesophagus and further. Topical antibiotics plus topical povidone-iodine daily may be sufficient, but surgical clean-up under a general anaesthetic may be needed.

Egg binding (Dystocia)

Egg-binding can occasionally be seen in adult females. Often it is secondary to another problem, such as obesity or lack of a suitable egg-deposition site. Distinct eggs-shaped swellings may be visible in the back half of the body or it may just appear swollen.

First approaches are to provide a correct environment including appropriate temperature, humidity and nesting chamber to help induce normal egg-laying. If this fails then consult your veterinarian, who can try to induce with oxytocin. There is only a small window of opportunity for its effective use – within 72 hours of obvious nesting or straining being seen. Do not be tempted to try to manipulate an egg out of the oviduct/cloaca – this should only be done under a general anaesthetic as it is a very delicate procedure, and there is a significant risk of trauma.

Neoplasia

Ball pythons, especially older individuals, are prone to develop a wide range of tumours.

Salmonella

Finally some general points on salmonellosis in reptiles. These bacteria are probably best considered as a normal constituent of lizard cloacal/gut microflora. They are rarely pathogenic to lizards but excretion is likely to increase during times of stress. In reality the risk to healthy hobbyists is minimal and infections in reptile owners are very rare. If isolated, treatment is usually not appropriate as it is unlikely to be effective long-term and may encourage antibiotic resistance.

Recommendations for prevention of salmonellosis from captive reptiles issued by the Center for Disease Control in the USA are:

- Pregnant women, children less than five years of age and persons with impaired immune system function (e.g. AIDS) should not have contact with reptiles.

- Because of the risk if becoming infected with Salmonella from a reptile, even without direct contact, households with pregnant women, children under five years of age or persons with impaired immune system function should not keep reptiles. Reptiles are not appropriate pets for child care centres.

- All persons should wash hands with soap immediately after any contact with a reptile or reptile cage.

- Reptiles should be kept out of food preparation areas such as kitchens.

- Kitchen sinks should not be used to wash food or water bowls, cages or vivaria used for reptiles, or to bath reptiles. Any sink used for these purposes should be disinfected after use.